P9-AQW-611

INTRODUCTION

Soccer is the world's most popular sport, but in America we are just beginning to embrace its charm. America's new love of soccer has not come from what you might have expected. The United States has not produced a soccer player with the talents of a Michael Jordan or a Tiger Woods. We did not invent the sport nor claim it as an American pastime. American's love for soccer came from the most unexpected of places. It grew in the hearts of young women. Women like Mia Hamm and Brandi Chastain, Tiffeny Milbrett and Julie Foudy. Soccer captivated these girls at an early age. They took their love for the sport and let it grow inside their hearts, until in one moment, they touched and captivated the hearts of us all. Their victory in the 1999 World Cup gave Americans their first glimpse of a sport that has long dominated the rest of the world. For the first time in history, women soccer players were gracing the covers of American magazines. They were interviewed in newspapers and appearing in prime time commercials. Women's soccer and American soccer were finally a topic of conversation for Americans everywhere. Although this soccer revolution seemed to start the moment Brandi Chastain's shot struck the back of the net, it had long been growing on the soccer fields of small towns and in the hearts of young girls.

SOCCER SKILLS & DRILLS

Skill Developing Games and Activities for Girls Six and Up

Stephen McGill

Wish
PUBLISHING

Wish Publishing
Terre Haute, Indiana
www.wishpublishing.com

Soccer Skills and Drills © 2005 Stephen McGill

All rights reserved under International and Pan-American Copyright Conventions.

No part of this book may be reproduced, stored in a data base or other retrieval system, or transmitted in any form, by any means, including mechanical, photocopy, recording or otherwise, without the prior written permission of the publisher.

LCCN: 2004118278

Editorial assistance provided by Amanda Burkhardt and Dorothy Chambers
Cover designed by Phil Velikan
Cover models: Natalie Napier, Courtney Sanzone, Amara Erickson and Holly Osburn
Cover photography by Holly Kondras and Phil Velikan
Interior artwork by Deborah Oldenburg and Phil Velikan

Printed in the United States of America
10 9 8 7 6 5 4 3 2 1

Published in the United States by
Wish Publishing
P.O. Box 10337
Terre Haute, Indiana 47801, USA
www.wishpublishing.com

Distributed in the United States by
Cardinal Publishers Group
Indianapolis, Indiana 46268

ACKNOWLEDGMENTS

I would like to thank several people for helping me complete this book. First, I want to thank my wife, Cinthia. Through her patience and love, I was able to find the time to write this book. I would also like to thank my father and John "Chappy" McGlachlan for instilling in me a love for the game. To my family and friends who have supported me through this process and to the Cambridge team of 2000, you have shown me what heart and determination can accomplish.

HOW TO USE THIS BOOK

Each page in this book represents a separate drill or activity. These pages expain how the drill is constructed, performed and monitored by the coach. The top of the page explains how the drill is performed and the basic rules that govern each component of the drill. The center of the page displays a detailed diagram of the drill itself. The bottom of the page contains three separate sections. These sections include key skills taught by the drill, coaching points and some alternatives to how the drill can be completed. Within every chapter there are drills that range from a beginning player's skill level to drills that require advanced soccer skills. The level of skill needed to complete a specific drill is located in the left or right margin of each individual drill's page. As teams and players improve, coaches can combine different levels of drills to ensure that the players are always challenged. The most effective practices will consist of drills from all three of the skill levels.

There are three separate skill levels listed in this book. They are Level 1, Level 2 and Level 3. If a drill is marked "For All," then players from all three skill levels can utilize these drills. Review the statements below to find which skill levels are best for your team.

SKILL LEVELS

Level 1: Beginners – These drills are designed to introduce fundamental skills to players who are new to the sport or to serve as a warm-up for more advanced players.

Level 2: Intermediate to advanced players – Players must have a good foundation in all technical areas to perform these drills. These drills can also be used in conjunction with either Level 1 or Level 3 drills.

Level 3: Advanced players only – The skills needed to perform these drills are substantial. Teams should not, however, overlook the first two skill levels based on their team's ability to complete Level 3 drills. The best opportunity to improve as both players and teams comes from using all three skill levels in combination with each other.

For All: These drills are for all three skill levels – These drills can be Level 1, Level 2, or Level 3 drills depending on the skill level of the players completing them.

MESSAGE FROM THE AUTHOR

When I decided to write this book, I did so with one thought in mind. How can I write one book that's beneficial to all the different coaches in the world? As we all know, every coach has his or her own style and beliefs on how to properly coach the sport of soccer. I am not looking to debate or compare with, or impose my coaching style on any of my colleagues. I do, however, want to contribute to helping coaches, players and teams get the most enjoyment out of the sport of soccer. I believe I have accomplished both of these goals with the information listed in the following pages. I hope you will enjoy reading this book as much as I have enjoyed writing it. I wish everyone a good practice and a great season.

— Stephen McGill

TABLE OF CONTENTS

CHAPTER I
DRIBBLING SKILLS

Every player on the field must be able to dribble the ball into space, beat an opponent with the dribble, and maintain possession of the ball. A player's ability to perform all of these skills is essential to the overall success of the team. Here you will find the drills to help you accomplish these goals.

Drill 1: Color Burst

Players wearing different colored practice vests dribble around inside a restricted area. Each color has the same number of players. The coach yells different actions for the players to complete. If the coach yells "same," the players must pair up with another player who is wearing the same-colored practice vest. The coach may also yell a combination of colors, "green, yellow," and the players wearing those colors must pair up one green and one yellow. The players wearing a color that has not been called should keep dribbling in the area. Coaches can change the commands any way they wish.

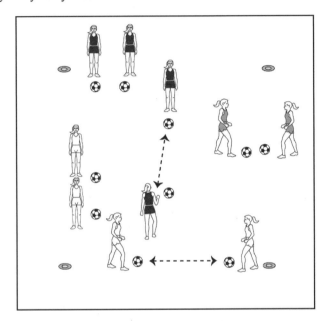

Setup: The size of the grid should be determined by the number of players participating in the drill. The more skilled the players, the less area they should be given to complete the drill.

Key skills learned: This drill is specifically designed to help improve the players' ability to dribble with the ball. Players must be able to dribble while avoiding other players, move with the ball in many different directions, and keep their heads up while dribbling.

Coach's corner: Coaches should avoid using any patterns when yelling their instructions. This will prevent players from teaming up prior to a command being called. Encourage the players not to be the last one to complete the command, but do not impose any penalties.

Alternatives to this drill: Coaches may come up with any number of color combinations to keep the players guessing.

Drill 2: Color Explosion

This is an expansion of the drill listed on the previous page. Players with different-colored practice vests are dribbling around inside the grid. The coach gives the command "red" and all the players wearing red vests must dribble around one of the outside cones and race back to the grid. The coach may also yell more than one color to keep all the players attentive. If more than one color is called, the players wearing those colors are to dribble their ball around one of the outside cones and return to the grid as fast as possible.

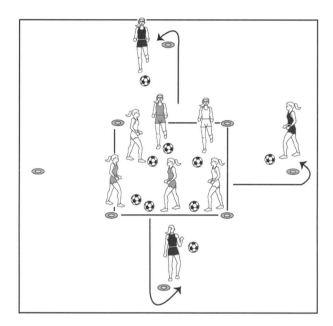

Setup: The center grid should be large enough to contain the number of players completing the drill. Place four cones 12 yards out from each side of the grid as shown in the diagram above.

Key skills learned: Players will practice dribbling the ball with speed. They must also concentrate on maintaining control of their ball inside the grid and be able to quickly locate the closest target cone. These conditions force the players to practice dribbling with their heads up.

Coach's corner: Mix up the calls to keep players from guessing the color of the next vest before it is called. You may also want to occasionally repeat a color. For example, if green just dribbled around the cone, call "green" again to keep players from losing concentration. Knowing that you may call players' colors even though they just completed their turn will keep them focused. Remember to encourage all the players not to be the last one back to the grid.

Alternatives to this drill: Add a defensive element to the drill. If the coach yells "green" then players not wearing green vests can leave their balls and try to prevent the green players, who are returning from the far cones, from dribbling back into the square.

Drill 3: Basic Dribbling

Line A: The first player dribbles with speed around the far cone and returns with the ball to the starting line. The second player takes the ball at the starting line and repeats the drill.

Line B: The first player weaves around the cones in a controlled dribbling exercise. The second player in line takes the ball from the first player and repeats the drill.

Line C: The coach teaches a dribbling move to the team and the player practices that move at each cone. The second player takes the ball from the first player and repeats the drill.

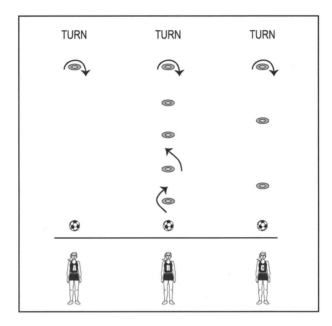

Setup: The skill level of the players completing the drill should determine the distances between the cones.

Key skills learned: Players will improve their ability to dribble the ball in different manners. This drill includes three dribbling styles: speed dribble, controlled weave, and dribbling moves to improve their one-on-one skills.

Coach's corner: Players should also practice using the outsides of their feet while performing the controlled weave and speed dribbling. Make sure each player is using both feet and not just the stronger of the two sides. Coaches can choose one or more of their favorite moves to practice in the moves portion of this drill.

Alternatives to this drill: Coaches can have teams compete in a relay for the speed dribbling or controlled weave portion of this drill. Set up separate lanes of cones and divide the players into groups. Teams complete the drill/relay at the same time. The first team that has all of its players complete the drill is the winning team.

Drill 4: Dribbling Square

The players will complete three stages of dribbling skills in this drill. The first stage is controlled dribbling. Players must control the ball as they weave in between several cones. The cut dribble is the second stage. Players use the inside and outside of their feet to cut the ball left or right in a 90-degree angle. The final stage is the speed dribble. Players dribble with pace without losing control of the ball. This drill should be continuous. The next player in line should begin the drill after the first player has finished the controlled-dribbling stage.

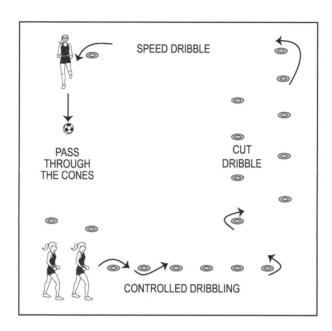

Setup: Place the cones as designed above.

Key skills learned: Players will learn to combine three different styles of dribbling. The first type of dribbling is the controlled weave, where players learn to dribble around obstacles. The second dribbling style is the cut dribble where players must "cut" the ball left or right. Finally, the player must dribble the ball with as much pace as possible. Players practice switching between styles without pausing and finish the drill with a skillful pass through the cones.

Coach's corner: It is important for the players to understand that in some situations it is better to be slower and efficient than fast but without control. The cut section of this drill must have the cones placed in a manner in which the player must actually be forced to cut the angle to the left or to the right in order to make the next cone. If the cones are placed too far in front of each other, then the player is really only doing a controlled weave drill.

Alternatives to this drill: Coaches can have teams race against the clock in a relay-style competition. Add 10 seconds to the overall time for each pass that does not go in between the cones.

Drill 5: Possession

The players dribble around inside of the 18-yard box and concentrate on not losing control of their balls. The coach yells for the players to complete a chosen dribbling move and the players must practice that move while dribbling. The coach may have the players practice as many moves as desired. The coach may also yell "end line" or "six-yard box" and force the players to move to those locations. The coach may also give the command to start a game called "possession." Each player must keep control of her ball while trying to kick the other players' balls outside of the 18-yard box. If a player's ball is kicked outside of the box, that player must retrieve her ball and either wait for the drill to finish or count to 20 before she can re-enter the drill.

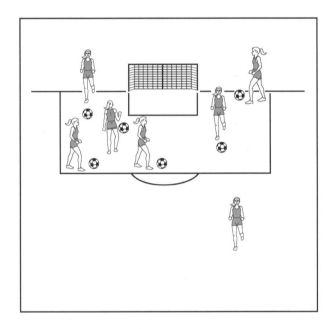

Setup: This drill is completed inside the 18-yard box.

Key skills learned: Players will improve their ability to dribble the ball in a confined area and practice making certain moves with the ball. During the game of possession, players must also practice shielding the ball from their opponents.

Coach's corner: Coaches should limit the number of moves taught to three or four a season. The players must practice a move for a given amount of time or they will not feel comfortable enough with it to use it during actual competition.

Alternatives to this drill: Coaches may also wish to play the possession game inside the 18-yard box. The coach will give the command for the game to begin. All the players inside the box will attempt to kick the other player's ball outside of the 18-yard box without losing possession of their own ball. Players are out of the game if their ball is kicked outside of the 18-yard box.

Drill 6: Quick Turns

Players practice different ways to turn with the ball. The players start the drill by dribbling to the first cone and turning to face the starting line. Players then dribble to the starting line and turn again to face the drill. Players continue to the second cone and so on until all four cones have been visited. Coaches decide which method or move the players are to use while completing this drill. Some suggestions are the "draw back," "the inside cut" and "the backwards roll" (see illustrations on page 8).

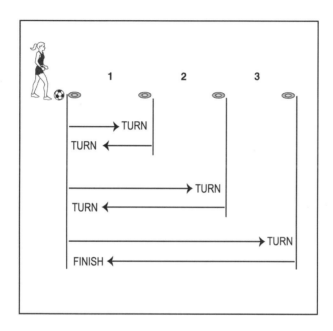

Setup: Cones need to be set up in a line with each cone being 10 yards past the cone before it. A line of cones on either end of the practice area will make it easier for all the players to be able to see where the next cone is located.

Key skills learned: Players practice different ways to turn with the ball. This skill is invaluable while dribbling to beat an opponent, dribbling to change the direction of attack, and for taking the ball away from congested areas.

Coach's corner: Players must be constantly in motion while completing this drill. The dribbling, turning, and then dribbling again need to be one motion and not three separate maneuvers. Split the team into two groups. While the first team is completing the drill, the second team can rest. Alternate groups until each group has completed the desired number of turns.

Alternatives to this drill: Practice the drill as designed.

Drill 7: Quick Turns

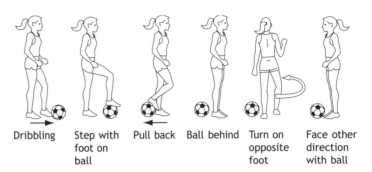

Dribbling | Step with foot on ball | Pull back | Ball behind | Turn on opposite foot | Face other direction with ball

Draw back: The player steps on the top of the ball and rolls it backward behind her. The player then turns on the pivot foot and faces the other direction with the ball at her feet.

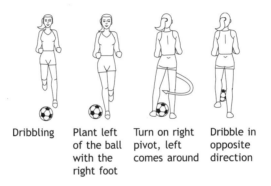

Dribbling | Plant left of the ball with the right foot | Turn on right pivot, left comes around | Dribble in opposite direction

Inside cut: The player steps beside the ball to one side and with the other foot cuts the ball back in the direction it came, while pivoting on the balance foot.

Dribbling | Step with foot on ball | Pull back | Whole body turns with ball | Right foot hits ground | Begin dribbling with the left foot

The roll: The player steps on the ball as in the draw back but this time turns with the ball as it is rolled in the opposite direction.

Drill 8: Who's Open

Two players begin the drill by dribbling their balls around the far cones. The first player to round the cone can pass to either of two waiting players. The second player must then pass to the remaining player. The players receiving the pass then dribble around the same cones as the passer. As the drill continues, the dribbling players will be forced to look up to find the player that is ready to receive the pass. The receiving players may have to dribble to either one of the cones depending on which player passes them the ball.

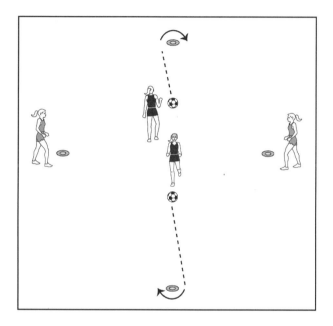

Setup: The far cones should be at least 15 yards away from the other players. This is the minimum distance for the drill to properly function.

Key skills learned: This drill is designed to teach beginning players how to look up while dribbling the ball. Players must keep the ball under control and turn with it while looking to make a pass to the open player.

Coach's corner: The stationary players must be ready to receive a pass from either side of the drill. Monitor the distance the players are keeping the ball while dribbling. Make sure that it is a controlled dribble and that the players are not just first touching the ball when it is halfway to the cones.

Alternatives to this drill: Practice the drill as designed.

Drill 9: Dribble Tag

Players dribble around inside a grid. There are two to three players who are "it." The "it" players must dribble their balls close enough to another player to be able to reach out and tag that player. If a player is tagged, she must stand with the ball over her head and spread her legs apart. The players who are not tagged can unfreeze a tagged player by passing their ball through the tagged player's legs. The player cannot be frozen again until her ball is back on the ground. The roles are switched when all players have been frozen. You may also want to play for a set amount of time and then switch the players who are "it."

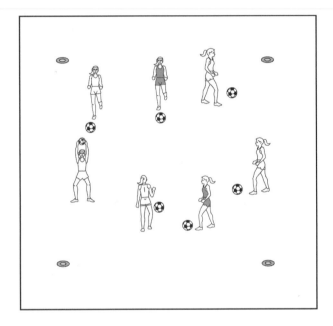

Setup: The size of the grid depends on the number of players participating in the drill.

Key skills learned: Players will improve their ability to dribble by practicing how to control the ball while being chased by another player. Players must also look up to see where the defense is located and be able to control their dribble in a confined area. Players will learn how to work together on offense and defense.

Coach's corner: The defense must work together in order to freeze all the offensive players. If the defense simply chases the players individually, they may never win the game. Offensive players must spread out as much as possible or one defensive player can freeze many offensive players in one area. To prevent injuries, advise the players only to tag below the shoulders. The "it" players can only tag a player if they are within playing distance of their own ball.

Alternatives to this drill: Remove the balls from the "it" players, but they must run backward while attempting to tag a player.

Drill 10: Chase

Players choose a partner and play a game of tag within the grid. Both players must dribble balls and have them within playing distance before tagging the other player. Once a player is tagged, the players switch roles. The players should stay in constant motion. If tagged, the tagged player immediately turns to chase the other player.

Setup: Coaches may set up the grid using cones or flags. You may also use the 18-yard box, center circle, or any other designated area on the field. The number of players and their skill level should help in determining the size of the playing area.

Key skills learned: Dribbling to control the ball is the main skill practiced in this drill. Players must learn to dribble the ball close to their bodies, keep their heads up, and be able to turn as needed with the ball at their feet. This drill is especially good for teaching players to dribble in congested areas.

Coach's corner: Dividing the team into two grids with the stronger players in one grid and the weaker players in the other will help facilitate learning. Make sure the partners are of equal skills to ensure that one player does not dominate the other.

Alternatives to this drill: Remove one ball from the pair and have the player without the ball face the player with the ball. The player with the ball then chases the other player around the grid while dribbling. The player without the ball must run backwards and face the dribbling player at all times. The coach yells "change" and the players, without stopping, switch roles.

Drill 11: Goals

The player with the ball is offense and the other player is a defender who attempts to steal the ball from the offensive player. If the defender steals the ball, that player becomes the offensive player. Goals are scored when a player dribbles the ball between the cones in either direction. Players compete for a set amount of time and record how many goals each has scored. The player who has scored the most goals is the winner of the drill.

Setup: Break the team up into two groups. While one group competes the other group can rest. Goals should be set up in many different directions.

Key skills learned: The focus of this drill is to improve the players' ability to beat an opponent with the dribble and to practice shielding the ball from the defender. The defender must practice taking the correct defensive stance while attempting to win the ball with a block or poke tackle.

Coach's corner: If possible, split the teams up into two groups. Run the first group for a minute and then let them rest as the second group completes the drill. Encourage the players to continue to play at a high level even as they get tired.

Alternatives to this drill: Practice the drill as designed.

Drill 12: One-on-One Plus Goals

Players compete against each other in this one-on-one dribbling contest. Goals are scored when either player passes the ball through the legs of her partner. If a goal is scored, the player pretending to be the goal then throws out a new ball and retrieves the ball that was just scored. Players compete for a set amount of time and then change positions with their partners.

Setup/rotation: Two players stand 15 to 20 yards apart with a ball in their hands and their legs spread open to create a goal for the offensive players. The center players start in between these "goal" players. Rotate the center players after a set amount of time.

Key skills learned: This drill helps players develop their one-on-one dribbling skills. Players must practice to improve their ability to take an opponent on with the ball. A skillful pass in between the legs of the "goal" is needed to score a point.

Coach's corner: The distance between the goals should be age specific. Older players need more space than younger players. Encourage the players to be creative when attacking the goal.

Alternatives to this drill: Coaches may allow the players to continue playing a ball that has gone behind the goal. Scoring from either side of the goal allows players to be more creative on the moves they choose to perform.

Drill 13: One-on-One to Goal

Players take turns going one-on-one with a defender. If the player is able to beat the defender, the player shoots on the goal. The defense must wait for the offensive player to pass between the cones before attempting to steal the ball.

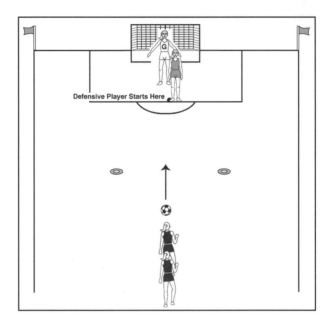

Setup/rotation: Form a single-file line about 30 yards out from the goal. The cones should be 10 yards in front of that line. Rotate the defender after a set amount of time.

Key skills learned: Players will practice beating an opponent while going to the goal. This drill also allows the defender to practice taking space from the offense, forcing the attacker one way, and winning the ball from the attacker.

Coach's corner: Dribbling around an opponent in an attempt to shoot is very different from beating an opponent in order to maintain possession. Players only need to gain a step or two to be able to take a clear shot. Encourage players to shoot at any opportunity they feel they might have. Some shots will get blocked, but the players will begin to learn the distance at which they can safely shoot the ball. Encourage the players to meet the defense with speed. The best way to get around a defender is by making one quick move and sprinting by them when they are off balance.

Alternatives to this drill: Using two goals side by side allows the players to get more opportunities to practice. Coaches may also add goalkeepers to make the drill more difficult and more like a game situation.

Drill 14: Change of Direction

Player (1) passes the ball to player (2) who then performs the "change-of-direction" (see page 16) and passes the ball to player (3). Player (3) finishes the drill by taking a shot on the goal.

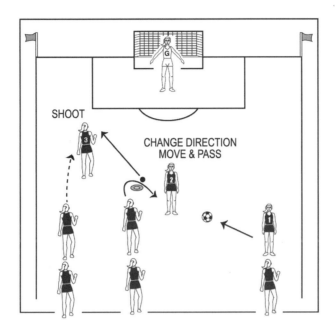

Setup/rotation: The lines should start far enough from the goal so that player (3) receives the ball at the corner of the 18-yard box. Rotate players so that (1) becomes (2), (2) becomes (3), and (3) becomes (1).

Key skills learned: Players will learn to quickly switch the field using a dribbling move. Moving the ball from side to side in a fast manner is key to attacking the defense. This move can also be used to dribble the ball away from a congested area.

Coach's corner: This particular move is speed dependent. If the ball is approaching the player with a lot of speed, then this is not the move to use. Make the players go through this drill slowly until they have mastered the move enough to practice it at full pace. The most important part of this drill is the ability to complete the move correctly and efficiently.

Alternatives to this drill: This drill can be switched to go to the right or the left. The drill can also be altered to have player (3) cross the ball to player (1).

Drill 15: Change-of-Direction Move

Approach the ball with the right foot out in front.

Ball goes between the legs.

Pivot on the left foot. Ball ends up on the outside of the left foot.

First touch in the other direction is with the outside of the left foot.

To do this move, the player fakes a touch with the right foot and allows the ball to roll in between her legs. The player then pivots with the left foot as the ball passes through her legs to the other side. The player touches with the outside of the left foot just as the ball starts to come out from under her.

Drill 16: Through-the-Legs Step Over

Player (1) passes the ball to player (2) as player (2) is running to a position ahead of player (1). Player (2) then completes the "through-the-legs step-over" (see page 18) and drop passes the ball back to player (1), who finishes with a shot on the goal.

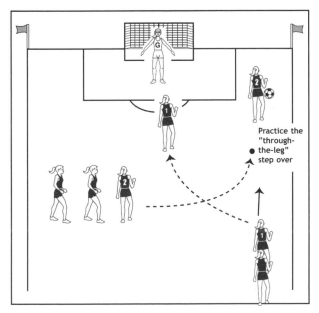

Setup/rotation: Start the drill 20 to 25 yards out from the goal. This will give player (2) enough space to complete the move and to drop pass to player (1). Rotate so that player (1) becomes player (2), and player (2) becomes player (1).

Key skills learned: Players will practice the "through-the-legs step over." Utilizing this dribbling move will allow players to quickly attack in the direction of choice. The quicker a player can receive the ball and take it from the direction it came to the direction she wishes to go, the better the player's chances of success.

Coach's corner: The player must control the ball with the foot nearest to the goal as it passes between her legs. This will prevent the ball from getting too far in front of the player. This slight touch will also change the direction of the ball enough to elude a defender that is closing in on the player.

Alternatives to this drill: This drill can be switched to go to the right or to the left. Player (1) can also go to a position to receive a cross instead of a drop pass.

Drill 17: The Step-Over Move

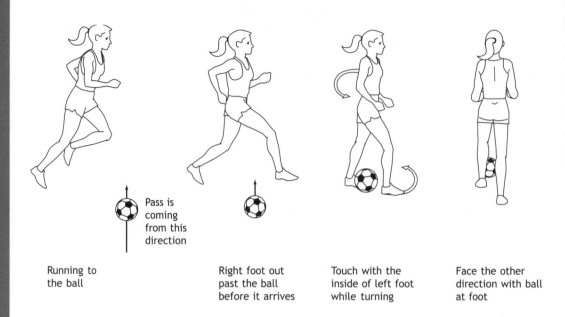

Pass is coming from this direction

Running to the ball

Right foot out past the ball before it arrives

Touch with the inside of left foot while turning

Face the other direction with ball at foot

The move is completed by stepping the right foot out past where the player thinks the ball is going to come, before it arrives, and then allowing the ball to pass in between her legs. As the ball is coming through her legs to the forward position, the player touches with the inside of her left foot. The player is now facing forward with the ball at her feet.

Drill 18: Confined Possession

Two players are confined inside a small grid. The offensive player practices shielding the ball from the defensive player for a set amount of time. No matter how many times the defensive player takes the ball, it is given back to the offensive player until the time has finished. After the time has elapsed, the players switch roles and begin the drill again.

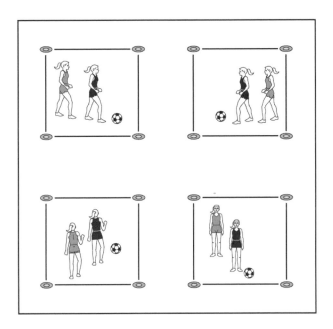

Setup/rotation: The grids are ten yards by ten yards. Rotate players from offense to defense after a given amount of time. Once both players have competed in both roles, switch one player to a new grid. Switching grids will allow players to compete against teammates of different skill levels.

Key skills learned: Being able to protect the ball is key in a player's ability to maintain possession. "Shielding" the ball is different from beating the player one-on-one or with moves. Shielding is used in small areas where the objective may not necessarily be to get around the player, but to prevent her from taking the ball or to take the position the player with the ball is occupying.

Coach's corner: Rotating the players from grid to grid is the best way to ensure that each player has a balanced experience during the drill. Rotating exposes different players to different techniques and dribbling styles. It also prevents a weaker player from being dominated by a better player the entire drill.

Alternatives to this drill: This drill can also be completed inside one large area. The players still compete one-on-one, but the other players form obstacles that each player must avoid.

Drill 19: One-on-One Plus Targets

Players compete in this one-on-one drill. Players attempt to score by passing the ball to the target players located at the end lines. The target players can move left and right to receive the pass. The offensive players must pass or dribble the ball to them to score a goal. The defense must attempt to steal the ball or block the pass to the target player. If the defensive player wins the ball, she then attempts to pass the ball to the opposite target player.

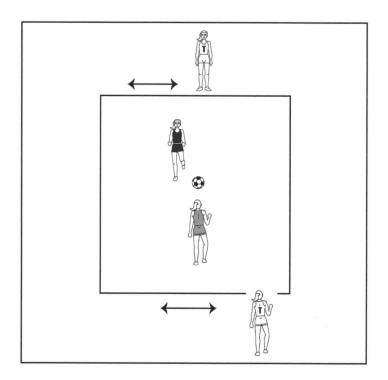

Setup/rotation: The field is 10 yards by 15 yards with two players on the inside and two target players on the outside. Rotate the target players with the players on the inside after a set amount of time.

Key skills learned: This drill is specifically designed to help improve individual dribbling skills. Players will practice dribbling to beat an opponent, maintaining possession of the ball, and shielding the ball from the defense. Players will also learn how to create a passing opportunity off the dribble.

Coach's corner: Players must become comfortable with having to beat opponents in a one-on-one situation. Explain that players should practice the moves they might use in games as well as try out new things. The more they practice and the more new moves they develop, the better they will be at beating defenders when the game begins. Keep things fair by grouping players according to their abilities.

Alternatives to this drill: When a player scores by passing the ball to the target player, allow the scoring player to keep possession of the ball and try to go back the opposite way through the grid to the other target player.

Drill 20: Left and Right Shielding

Players tuck two ribbons inside the waistband of their shorts or pants. One ribbon is placed on each side of the body. Players dribble around inside the grid and attempt to steal the ribbons off the other players. If a player loses both ribbons, she is out of the game.

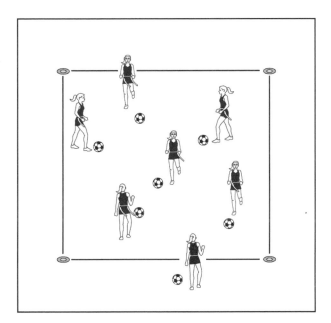

Setup: Cut strips of cloth into 12 inch-long by 2 inch-wide ribbons. Make sure the players only tuck four inches into their clothing.

Key skills learned: This drill forces players to learn to shield the ball with both sides of their body.

Coach's corner: The players are going to lose one ribbon at a time. That forces the player to concentrate on keeping the side of the body with the ribbon on it away from the other players. Players must now dribble with the foot on the same side as the ribbon and shield the ball with the side of the body that has already lost the ribbon. Players will not be able to choose which foot they want to dribble with, and will have to work on their weak side at least half of the time.

Alternatives to this drill: Practice the drill as designed.

CHAPTER 2
PASSING THE BALL

There is no substitute for the ability to make good passes on the soccer field. No other aspect of soccer has as much impact on the outcome of a game as good passing. A team with limited individual skills but the ability to move the ball around the field effectively can overcome its individual weaknesses to beat a stronger team.

Drill 1: The Gauntlet

Players run through a "gauntlet" where they must pass the ball back to the players on either side of the lane. Players need to make their passes go between the cones. Players can receive the first pass from either the right or the left and then turn to receive the second pass from the opposite side. When the players have completed their last pass they return to the back of the line.

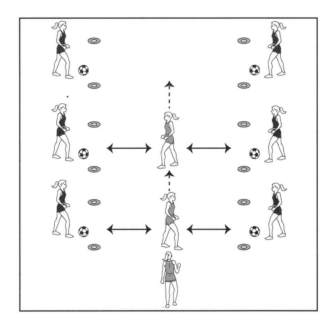

Setup/rotation: Six sets of cones are set up an equal distance apart from each other. A player stands one yard behind each set of cones. Rotate by changing all the passers in the "gauntlet" after a set amount of time.

Key skills learned: This is an excellent passing drill for beginners. Players get to make several passes in a short amount of time. This drill can also be altered to practice a variety of different skills (see the alternatives listed below).

Coach's corner: The players should move through this drill at a fast pace, but it is important that they make good passes and not just quickly hit the ball in the general direction of the passer. This is why the cones are marked on the field and the "gauntlet" players are standing one yard behind the cones. Players should pass the ball back through these cone "goals."

Alternatives to this drill: Instead of passing the ball, the players can practice trapping the ball or heading the ball back to the thrower. Players may also practice the "change-of-direction move". The players allow the ball to roll through their open legs and quickly turn to face the opposite direction. Only one ball per "gauntlet" pair is needed for practicing the "change-of-direction move." The directions for this move are located on page 16.

Drill 2: Token Wall Passing

Two players begin 10 to 12 yards apart and wall pass around "active," but not "determined" defenders. Each team should face three to four defenders and finish with a shot on the goal. Defenders should take the ball if the pass is not good, but should not move more than one yard from their positions.

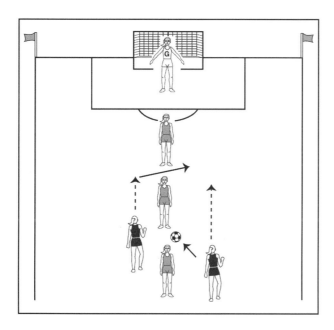

Setup/rotation: Placing cones where you want the defenders to stand will keep them from crossing the passing lanes and the distance between the defenders. Rotate the defensive players after a set amount of time.

Key skills learned: This drill allows the players to practice the distance at which a wall pass should be made around a defender.

Coach's corner: This is a basic example for the players to understand the concept of wall passing. It teaches them not to wait too long before making the pass and to keep moving in support of the player who has just received the ball. Increase the speed of the drill as the skill level increases. This drill is designed for beginners.

Alternatives to this drill: Practice the drill as designed.

Drill 3: Slot Passing

Players pass the ball through a set of cones to a player waiting two yards behind the cones. The receiving player then turns and passes through a second set of cones and so on down the line. The last player receives the pass and turns to shoot on the goal.

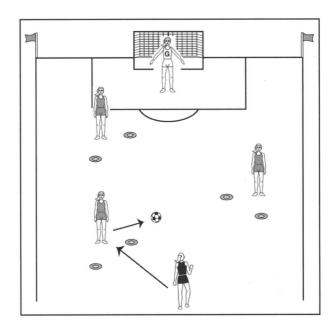

Setup: The placement of the cones is essential in this drill. You want to make sure the players have space to receive the pass and to take two or three dribbles before passing to the next pair of cones. The player that shoots on the goal returns to the back of the line and begins the drill again.

Key skills learned: This drill allows the players to practice the speed and accuracy of their passes. They must also receive the ball, look up to find the next target, and pass within a short amount of time. Players will begin to learn to control the ball in the direction of the next pass.

Coach's corner: It is important to actually mark the receiving players' passing lanes with the cones. You can use just one cone to mark the position of the receiving player, but I have found that players concentrate more if they have a "goal" or target area into which they must pass the ball. Demonstrate to the players that controlling the ball in the direction of the next pass will increase the time they have to make the pass.

Alternatives to this drill: This drill can be done in many different ways.

1. Receiving players can wall pass back to a single player who is completing the drill by running through the center of the area and passing left and right.

2. The first player can pass and follow to take up the position of the first receiver and so on down the line.

3. This drill can be just a passing drill, or the player can finish the drill with a shot on the goal.

Drill 4: Power Passing to Space

Players pair up and practice finding space in a confined area. One player operates in each zone and partners cannot cross the center line. The players must move around and create space for each other in order to pass the ball back and forth. Players need to use the whole area including depth. If a partner is not open then the player should practice dribbling through the traffic created by the other players. During the drill, the coach is to yell "hold." This means that whoever has the ball at that time needs to protect it from the players who do not have a ball. If the ball is kicked out of the zone it is out of play. The last player who is still in possession of a ball is the winner.

Setup: The size of the zone will depend on how many players are present and the skill level of the players involved.

Key skills learned: This drill teaches the players how to find the open spaces, search the area for an open player (their partner), and make passes through congested areas.

Coach's corner: Players need to be moving left and right, forward and backward through their zones. Do not let them stay on one side of the area or run just across the lines from each other. The more movement and depth they practice with, the better they will learn from the drill.

Alternatives to this drill: Coaches can change the number of players to form teams of three or four. You may also remove a ball from a team. This team is now the defense and must attempt to steal a pass from another partnership or team. If the defense successfully steals a ball, then they are now offensive players again. The team that had the ball stolen must now steal one for itself. Balls may be stolen only on passes and not from a dribbling player.

Drill 5: Left and Right Touch Passing

Players form a straight line in front of one player designated as the "passer." Player (1) begins the drill by dribbling forward two to five yards and then passing either to the left cone or to the right cone depending on where the passer is running. The passer must run to the cone and make a touch pass back to player (1) who finishes the drill with a shot on the goal.

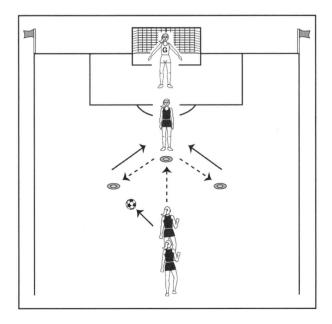

Setup/rotation: Cones need to be set up in a triangle formation about 25 yards out from the goal. The distance between the cones of the triangle should be eight to 10 yards. Rotate the passer after a set amount of time.

Key skills learned: Sometimes in the game there are moments when players find themselves in front of a teammate who is dribbling the ball straight to where they are standing. Players often seem confused about where to move. They need to either help the player with the ball or clear a path for her to continue down the field. This drill teaches the players to recognize this situation to have a built-in plan for turning the moment into an opportunity to pass the ball.

Coach's corner: Forwards are most likely to find themselves in the situation listed above. I would suggest using the team's forwards as the passers in this drill.

Alternatives to this drill: Practice the drill as designed.

Drill 6: The Arch Warm-Up

Three players are positioned in a triangle formation. The active player practices making one-touch passes to the other two players. The active player passes on one side, retreats around the cone and receives a pass from the other side. The active player is then rotated out after a set amount of time.

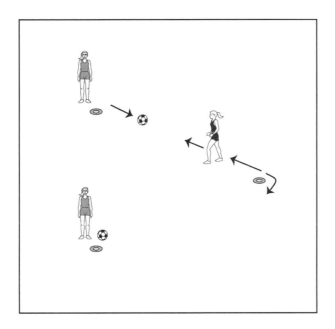

Setup/rotation: Three cones are set in a triangle formation about 15 yards from each other. Change the active player after a set amount of time.

Key skills learned: Players will practice one-touch passing while completing this drill. Players will also learn to concentrate on their skills while playing at a high work rate.

Coach's corner: One-touch passing demands that the players coordinate timing, positioning, contact and the follow through in order to successfully pass the ball. Monitor the players and help those who need to improve one or more of these aspects. Players must be able to one-touch pass to be successful on the soccer field.

Alternatives to this drill: Practice the drill as designed. The two outside players may toss the ball to the active player and force her to trap the ball before passing it back. Players may also be asked to head the ball to the throwers.

Drill 7: One-Touch Drop

Set up two lines of players and mark, with cones, a second line five yards behind the players on both sides. The objective is for the players to pass to their partner across from them, retreat back to the second line, and run forward to receive the next pass back at the original line. This is continuous for both players. Time the passes so that the player receives the ball at the same time she is returning to the first line.

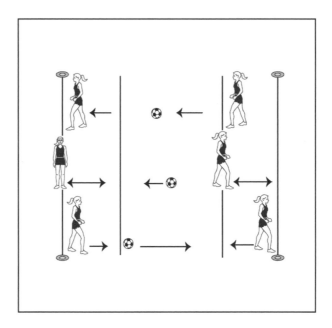

Setup: The passing distance should be 10 yards apart with five yards marked out behind each line.

Key skills learned: This drill allows the players to practice the pace and timing of their passes. They must adjust to the distance and speed of their partner's pass to make a good return pass.

Coach's corner: The ideal pass for this drill will meet the player at the line as she returns from the back line. The ball must be hit with the appropriate amount of pace to get the timing right.

Alternatives to this drill: Practice the drill as designed.

Drill 8: Grid Wall Passing

Players form a partnership. One player dribbles the ball and the other runs freely throughout the grid. The player with the ball passes to her partner. The partner then wall passes back to the player. This process is repeated throughout the area of the grid. Players need to adjust their passes so as not to be interrupted by the other players in the grid.

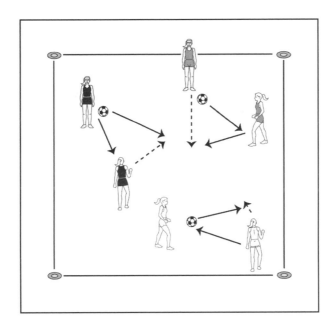

Setup/rotation: The grid needs to allow enough space for the players to complete their passes. However, if there is room for the teams to complete their passes without having to adjust to the positions of the other players, then the size of the grid is too large. Rotate which partner has the ball after a set amount of time.

Key skills learned: Players must practice setting up and completing wall passes in this drill. The players must coordinate with their partners to find the space necessary to complete the wall passes.

Coach's corner: Players will have more success if they spread out and make runs toward each other. Try to prevent players from running side by side and simply passing back and forth. Instruct the players to make the passes out in front of their partners to make it easy to get a return pass.

Alternatives to this drill: Eliminate the partnership and allow the players with the balls to wall pass with any available player.

Drill 9: Quick Passing

Players practice making different types of passes. Player (1) starts with the ball and makes a long pass to player (2). Player (2) then wall passes the ball back to player (1). Player (1) makes a short pass to player (3) who then passes it back to the starting line.

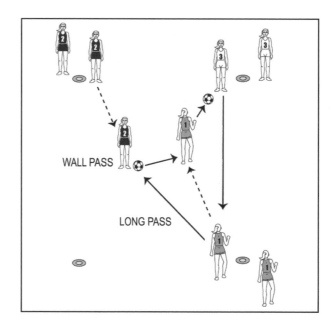

Setup/rotation: Make a grid with the dimensions of 15 yards wide by 25 yards long. Rotate the players so that (1) becomes (3), (3) becomes (2) and (2) becomes (1).

Key skills learned: Several different types of passes are practiced in this drill. Through repetition players improve their ability to wall pass, and make short and long passes to open players.

Coach's corner: Monitor the passes to ensure that the players pass the ball in front of the receiving players. Also, check to see that the appropriate amount of pace is put on these passes. Players should not have to wait for the ball or try to control a ball that is struck with too much force.

Alternatives to this drill: Practice the drill as designed.

Drill 10: Move to Receive

Place cones in a line about 15 to 20 yards apart from each other. The closest cone to the starting line is empty. The starting player passes the ball to the empty cone which forces player (1) to run to it to receive the pass. Player (1) wall passes back to the starting player and the second pass is made to the empty second cone. This forces the next player to run to the second cone and so on down the line. When the player receives the last wall pass they take a shot on the goal.

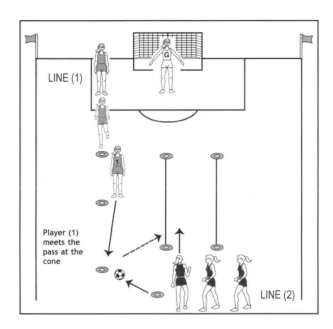

Setup/rotation: Make sure there is a target passing lane set up as shown above. This will keep the players from increasing or decreasing their passing distance. Rotate player (1) to the back of line (2) and rotate players in line (2) to the start of the cones in line (1). The goalie will punt the ball back to line (2).

Key skills learned: This drill teaches the players how to come to the ball and receive a pass instead of waiting for the ball to come to them. They must also practice passing the ball back to the player while they are still in motion. This is much different than a stationary pass.

Coach's corner: Coaches must designate how large a passing lane the players will have while completing this drill. If no lane is designated then the players will spread out too far or come too close to the passers and they will lose the benefit of this drill. Do not attempt this drill if your goalie is a weak punter. This is good practice for the goalies if they can already punt the ball. Do not have them learn to punt with this drill. The rotation of the drill is based on the goalie's ability to clear the ball out to the starting line.

Alternatives to this drill: This drill can be run from the left or the right side of the field.

Drill 11: Numbered Passing

Two teams of four complete this drill inside a confined area. All of the players must constantly be moving throughout the grid. The teams work independently from each other, but must be aware of the other team's players. The objective for each team is to move around the area and complete passes in a sequential order. Player (1) passes to player (2), player (2) passes to player (3) and so on. Players must move around the area to receive passes from the appropriate numbered player. The groups are not separated in space so they must be constantly moving to get out of the other team's way.

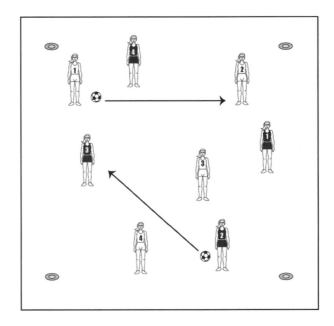

Setup: There should be enough room for all the players to move around the grid. If the teams have too much space and are able to separate from each other, then reduce the size of the grid.

Key skills learned: Players are forced to move into space, look for the open player, and make good passes to complete this drill. This drill is as much of a thinking drill as it is physical exercise. Players have to constantly keep track of where their teammates are and where the next pass needs to go. This type of thinking will help them see things faster in the games.

Coach's corner: Communication is key for the players completing this drill. If they do not speak to each other, they will not be able to complete the drill in a quick manner. This type of delay can cause missed opportunities in the games and loss of ball possession.

Alternatives to this drill: Coaches can have the players go in reverse order, or once player (4) receives the ball, she must pass backwards to player (1). The rules may also be changed to allow a player on the other team to steal a pass from the other group as long as that player does not miss her own team's passing order.

Drill 12: Three-Man Weave

Players must perform a three-man weave through a confined area. Players simply pass to the left or right and run around the player receiving the ball. Use the cones to keep the players from spreading out too much. Players can finish with a shot on the goal, or they can simply double the drill as shown in the diagram below. Players should form a line at the start of the second set of cones. Do not expect the players to turn while doing the three-man weave.

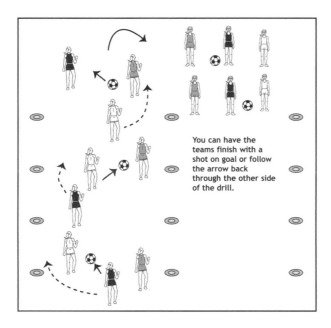

You can have the teams finish with a shot on goal or follow the arrow back through the other side of the drill.

Setup: The skill level of the players should determine the distance between the cones. Better players need to be able to pass the ball in a smaller area.

Key skills learned: This drill teaches the players how to pass efficiently in a small area of play. The players will also become better at leading the target player with the pass and making supporting runs after the ball has been played.

Coach's corner: Coaches must designate how large a passing lane the players will have while completing this drill. If there is not a designated area, the players will spread out so much that they will lose the benefit of this drill.

Alternatives to this drill: The teams can stay in one lane and finish with a player taking a shot on goal or line up after the turn and repeat the drill by coming back through a second set of cones.

Drill 13: Short, Short, Long

Several groups of three players run inside a defined area. These players must make two short passes and then one long pass. It does not matter which two players make short passes and which player receives the long pass. These positions will rotate throughout the drill.

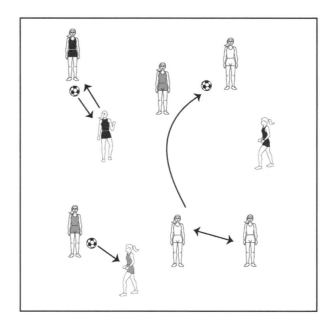

Setup: Coaches need to define the size of the area in which the players must complete this drill. The size of the area should be determined by the number and skill level of the players completing this drill.

Key skills learned: The players must use many different skills to be able to complete this passing drill. The players must be able to find the open player, pass long distances with accuracy, and make supporting runs to the player who has just received the ball.

Coach's corner: Players will slowly begin to make shorter runs during this drill. The shorter the long pass, the less distance the players need to run for a supporting pass. To prevent players from making three short passes instead of completing the drill as it is designed, coaches need to make sure that all long passes are at least 15 yards. This will help the players maintain a good cardiovascular workout as well as improve their passing ability.

Alternatives to this drill: Coaches can dictate how the long passes should be made. Some examples include:

1. All long passes are to be in the air.
2. All long passes need to be struck with the outside of the foot.
3. All long passes are "chip" shots over the first player's head.

Drill 14: Line Short, Short, Long

This drill is the stationary version of the drill on the previous page. Teams of three players position themselves in a line across the field. The two outside players should be no further than 30 yards apart. The drill begins with a short pass from player (1, white) to player (2, black). Player (2)then returns the pass to player (1) and player (1) makes a long pass to player (3, grey). Player (2) must run to take up a supporting position for player (3). Player (3) receives the ball and makes a short pass to player (2). Player (2) makes a short pass back to player (3) and the whole process is repeated.

Setup/rotation: The outside players need to be no more than 30 yards apart. The middle player should stay at least eight yards from the outside players. This allows space for the outside players to strike the ball over the middle player's head. Rotate the middle player after a set amount of time.

Key skills learned: This drill helps players practice kicking long passes. It also combines several different skills to make it more like a game situation. Players must control the ball from a long pass, make a pass to a supporting player, and one-touch the long pass to the open player who is down the field. This drill is also a cardiovascular workout for the player in the middle position.

Coach's corner: Monitor the passes to make sure the players receiving the long pass do not have to move a great distance to meet the ball. The ideal pass will land at the players' feet. The short passes from the middle player must be kept on the ground to give the players who are striking the long pass the best situation in which to strike the ball accurately.

Alternatives to this drill: Practice the drill as designed.

Drill 15: Five-on-Two

Five players attempt to score goals on two defenders. A goal is scored when the five players cross the end line with the ball in control and at their feet. The player that dribbles across the "goal" line then turns and faces the grid. The offensive players then attack the defense in the other direction.

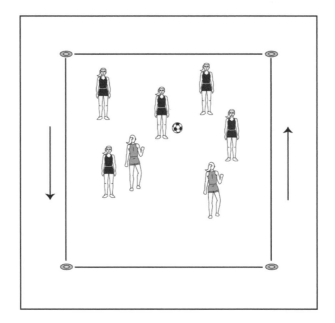

Setup/rotation: Set up a grid that measures approximately 15 by 25 feet. Rotate players from offense to defense after a set amount of time.

Key skills learned: Short passing around defenders is the main skill practiced in this drill. Players may also work on fakes or moves to disguise their passes.

Coach's corner: This is a classic drill that has been practiced for years, but its advantages are obvious. Coaches need to be sure the players are skillful enough to be able to pass with one or two touches. Beginning players and some intermediate players will not be able to complete this drill in a manner that is beneficial.

Alternatives to this drill: Have the five players form a circle around the two defenders. The idea is to pass around the circle without the defense intercepting the ball. There are several ways to decide who changes from offense to defense.

1. Players change after a set amount of time.
2. The defender who intercepts the pass moves to the outside.
3. The player who has been in the center the longest moves to the outside after a stolen or bad pass.

CHAPTER 3
IMPROVING YOUR SHOT

A team can do everything right on the field, but if the ball does not hit the back of the net, that team may lose the game. This chapter contains different setups and drills to give the players more practice and experience in taking shots on the goal.

Drill 1: Pure Shooting

Players attack two different goals in this shooting drill. Player (1) passes the ball to player (2) of their line. Player (2) then wall passes it to player (1) for a shot on the goal. Player (1) then becomes the wall passer and player (2) retrieves the ball and goes to the back of the other line. Both lines rotate in this manner.

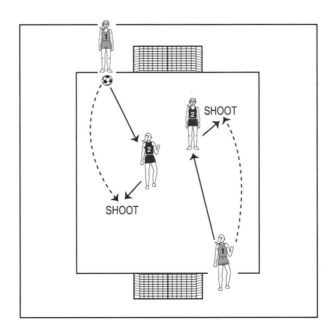

Setup/rotation: Two goals should be set up to face each other 40 yards apart. The wall passers, player (2), should start inside the field and 15 to 20 yards out from their teams' goals. Rotate player (1) to player (2). The old player (2) is responsible for getting the ball and returning to the back of the next line.

Key skills learned: Players will practice striking the ball on the goal in this fast-paced drill. The approach, contact and follow through will be practiced repeatedly to help develop the players' shooting ability.

Coach's corner: First, have the players concentrate on striking the ball correctly. Once the players can correctly hit the ball, focus on where the balls are being placed into the goal. When the players are consistent and accurate, increase the power slowly until the player can strike the ball with pace and not sacrifice accuracy.

Alternatives to this drill: The drill can easily be switched to work the left foot by having the lines move to the opposite side of the goals.

Drill 2: Line Shooting

A player stands 25 yards out from the goal. Two shooters pass the ball to the player and run to the right or the left side of her. The player wall passes the ball back to the shooter who finishes the drill with a shot on the goal.

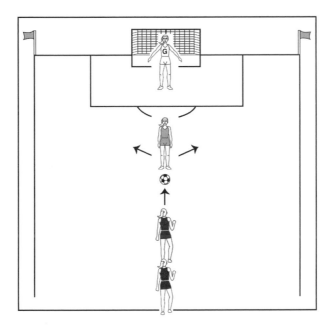

Setup/rotation: Set up the drill as diagramed above. After the player shoots, she will get the ball and return to the back of the line.

Key skills learned: This is a pure shooting drill to help the player become better at striking the ball.

Coach's corner: Passes need to be out in front of the players to allow them to adjust to the ball and take a good shot. The focus should be on the player's technique and not whether the player scores. Take the time to correct any wrong techniques or motions.

Alternatives to this drill: The passes back to the players can be lifted to make them practice shooting a bouncing ball.

WESTCHESTER PUBLIC LIBRARY CHESTERTON, IN

Drill 3: Obstacle Shooting

Two lines start 30 yards out from the goal. The players must complete a controlled-dribbling portion of the drill and then take a shot on the goal.

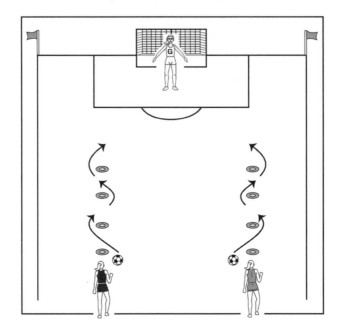

Setup/rotation: The lines will alternate when completing this drill. The first player in each line starts the drill when the player in the other line is finished with the controlled-dribbling section. After the players have taken their shot, they will rotate to the back of the opposite line.

Key skills learned: Players will seldom get an open shot in a game situation without having to beat a defender before striking the ball. This drill helps the players learn to set up their shot before the last defender has been beaten.

Coach's corner: Only one player is actively shooting at the goal at a given moment. This allows the goalie to play both lines. Players should be instructed to hit the shot immediately after passing the last cone. Do not let players take three to five touches past the cone. In a game situation the player may only have an open shot for a second before it is gone.

Alternatives to this drill: Coaches may wish to have both lines completing the drill simultaneously while two goalies share the responsibility of guarding the goal. Designate one goalie for each half of the goal. A second goal may also be set up to have four lines completing the drill at the same time.

Drill 4: Fast Shot

The coach stands inside the goal while the players complete the drill. The player begins the drill from the end line and runs around the first cone. While the player is turning, the coach rolls a ball toward the first cone. The coach needs to roll the ball so the player has two to three yards to adjust to it after she comes around the cone. The ball must be thrown before the player gets to the cone. Once the player has taken the shot, she must turn and run around the second cone. Again, the coach needs to time the throw to arrive just after the player comes around the cone. The player takes five shots and the drill is reset for the next player.

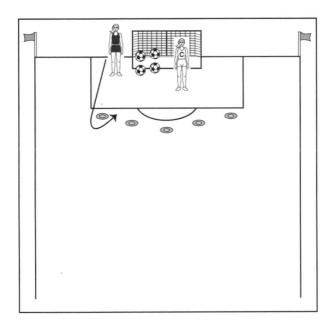

Setup: Position the cones as shown in the diagram above.

Key skills learned: This is a pure shooting drill that improves the players' ability to strike a ball on the run. Players will be asked to strike the ball on their first touch. This is much different than shooting off the dribble and requires more concentration on timing.

Coach's corner: The throw is most important for this drill to work properly. The player should strike the ball almost immediately after rounding the cone. Take time after each player completes the course to correct any mistakes in her shooting technique.

Alternatives to this drill: Vary the throws to make the player adjust to different circumstances. The first throw is on the ground, the second throw is bouncing, etc.

Drill 5: Heading to Goal

The coach stands to the side of the goal and tosses balls for the players to head into the goal. The players are encouraged to head the ball low to the ground and into the corners.

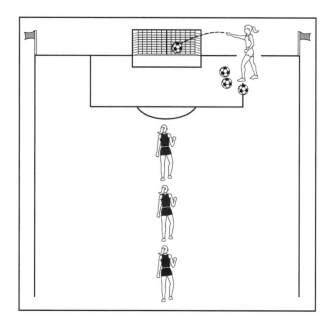

Setup: Set up drill as diagramed above.

Key skills learned: Players will simulate heading the ball into the goal from a corner kick or a cross.

Coach's corner: Start with tosses that are high and allow the player to get underneath them without rushing. This will give the players enough time to concentrate on the proper mechanics of heading the ball. If your players are highly skilled, then vary your tosses to make them adjust to the ball. Advise players on their location to the goal and what is the highest percentage shot from that location.

Alternatives to this drill: Coaches may also want to place target cones inside the goal. This helps players to visualize where the ball needs to be placed. This drill can also be used to practice volleys.

Drill 6: Turn and Shoot

Two players in the front of each line stand five yards out from the remaining players. These two players face the second player in each line. The second player passes the ball to the first player. The first player quickly turns with the ball and shoots on goal. Lines should alternate turns to prevent two players from shooting at the same time.

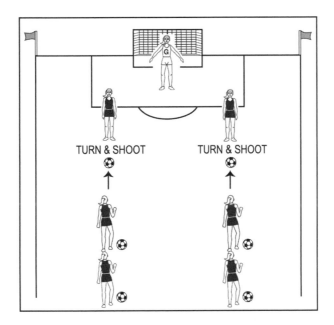

Setup/rotation: Set up the drill as diagramed above. Rotate the players in line by having the passer become the shooter. After a player shoots the ball, she moves to the back of the opposite line.

Key skills learned: This drill is specifically designed to help improve the speed in which the player can receive the ball, turn and shoot on the goal.

Coach's corner: You can either give the players a certain turning maneuver you want them to use or simply critique the maneuvers the players use on their own. Remind the players that the faster they can face the goal, the better scoring opportunity they will have.

Alternatives to this drill: The passing player can toss the ball and force the shooter to trap the ball before turning to shoot.

Drill 7: Opportunistic Scoring

The coach or a player simulates a bad goal kick. The players must bring the ball under control quickly and shoot on the goal.

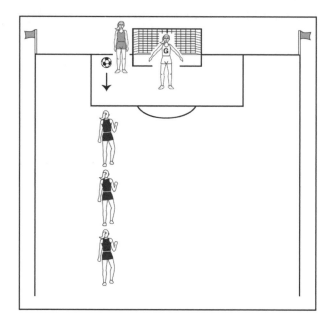

Setup: The coach or player should use the end line as the kicking point. This will allow the goalie to see the shot coming toward the goal. It will also prevent the coach or player from being hit by the shot.

Key skills learned: Players will simulate receiving the ball from a bad clear or goal kick. Too often players do not get the ball under control fast enough to get the shot away. In this drill, players will practice bringing the ball down and getting the shot off as quickly as possible.

Coach's corner: The key to scoring in this situation is keeping the ball in front of the players. The players need to understand that even if the trap is not a good one, at the minimum, they need to keep the ball in front.

Alternatives to this drill: If the team has two goalies, you can have two lines completing this drill at the same time, one line on the left side and one line on the right side of the goal. Two goals may also be set up side by side to increase the number of players actively completing the drill.

Drill 8: Quick Shot

The first player in the line stands with her back toward the goal. The goalie passes a ball out to the first player. Before the ball arrives, the goalie yells "turn" and the player turns to the ball and shoots at the goal.

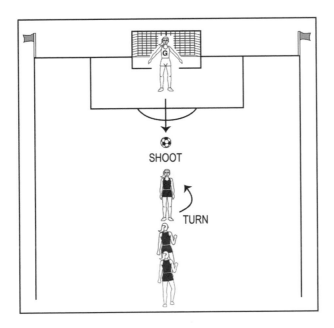

Rotation: Once the first player has taken the shot, the second player walks out and becomes the shooter. The player who shoots then goes to the back of the line.

Key skills learned: This drill will help players learn to adjust quickly to a shooting opportunity.

Coach's corner: Limit the time a player has to react to the ball by calling "turn" just before the ball arrives at the player. The quicker a player can turn, locate the ball and shoot, the better chance she has of scoring the goal.

Alternatives to this drill: Passes can be straight down the middle of the field or to the right or the left of the player. You can also throw a high ball or bounce it off the ground to make it more like a game situation.

Drill 9: Dummy Runs

Player (1) dribbles the ball to the cone and then crosses the ball to player (2). Player (2) fakes the shot or "dummies" the ball and lets it pass to player (3). Player (3) finishes the drill with a shot on the goal.

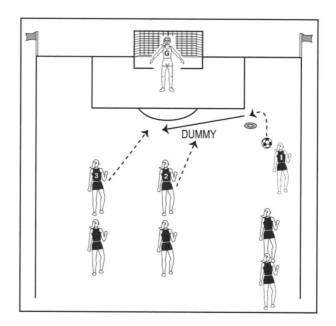

Setup/rotation: Place one cone three yards out from the corner of the 18-yard box. Rotate players so that (1) becomes (2), (2) becomes (3) and (3) becomes (1).

Key skills learned: Players will improve their ability to create shooting opportunities by making dummy runs to the ball. They will also improve their shooting reaction time or the amount of time it takes them to get a shot toward the goal. Finally, the players will gain experience in shooting a ball that is coming from their side instead of directly in front of them.

Coach's corner: There are two main areas to focus on in this drill. The first is the cross from player (1). The cross needs to be hit with some speed. The ball needs to go past player (1) and be able to reach player (2) before the defense has time to react. The second area of concern is the believability of the "dummy" move. The player has to make it real enough to fool the defender, or the defender will just react to the ball and the offense may lose a good scoring opportunity.

Alternatives to this drill: This drill can also be used to improve your goalie's reaction time. Change the drill to allow players (2) and (3) to decide who will shoot the ball. Maybe player (2) will dummy the shot or maybe she will take the shot. Not knowing who is shooting will force the goalie to adjust immediately to any shot coming toward the goal.

Drill 10: Drop-Pass Scoring

Player (3) passes the ball to player (1) who is running across the field. Player (1) receives the ball and dribbles across the top of the 18-yard box. Player (2) circles behind player (1) and receives a drop pass from her. Player (2) then shoots on the goal.

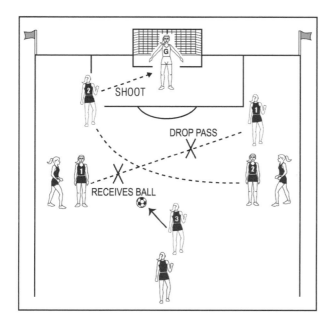

Setup/rotation: The three lines should be set up 15 to 20 yards from each other in a triangle formation. Rotate players so that (3) bcomes (1), (1) becomes (2) and (2) becomes (3).

Key skills learned: Players practice creating a shot at the top of the 18-yard box. This take-over/drop pass play will give the players an open shot in a game situation. The drill will help players learn to be aware of those around them and that coordinating with these players may help to create a shooting opportunity.

Coach's corner: Players will need direction on how far apart to make the run from each other and when to make the drop pass. Helping them with this timing is essential in their understanding of how this play works.

Alternatives to this drill: This drill can be run from the right or the left by simply changing the first pass to go to either player (1) or player (2).

Drill 11: Reaction Shooting

The first player faces the goal while the second player in the line tosses the ball over the first player's head. The first player must adjust to the ball, get the ball under control, and shoot on the goal. The second player replaces her and the drill is repeated.

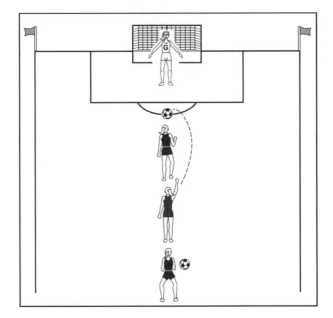

Rotation: The player who shoots the ball will go to the end of the line. The player who just tossed the ball moves forward and becomes the shooter.

Key skills learned: This drill is specifically designed to help improve the speed in which a player can locate the ball, bring it under control, and take a shot on the goal.

Coach's corner: Tosses need to be within five yards of the player. This forces the player to control a bouncing ball. If the tosses are too long, the player is simply running in behind a rolling ball.

Alternatives to this drill: Tosses may be straight down the center or to the left or right side of the player. You may also have the shooters lie down on the ground and get up after the balls are tossed over their heads. This simulates getting knocked down in the box or on the field where no call was made and the ball is still near the player.

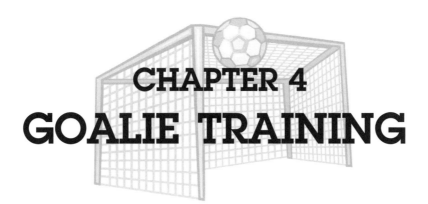

CHAPTER 4
GOALIE TRAINING

Most of the drills in this book end with a shot on the goal. This chapter, however, contains drills specifically designed to help goalies improve their reflexes and timing.

Drill 1: Goal to Goal

Two goalies face off in a drill designed to improve upper body mobility. The two goalies sit on their bottoms and face each other. The objective is for the goalies to score goals by throwing the ball below the head and in between the cones. Coaches can decide how many goals constitute a drill. Players must stay with their bottoms on the ground and their feet out in front of them, even when throwing the ball. The only time the bottom and legs can come off the ground is during a dive or lean to the left or the right.

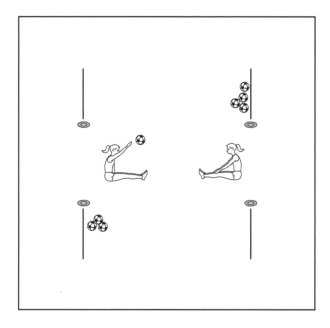

Setup: The goals need to be just wider than the reach of the goalie. The distance from one goal to the next should be determined by the size and strength of the players.

Key skills learned: This drill will improve the players' ability to dive to the left and right sides. The upper body will also become more flexible since it must compensate for not having movement in the lower part of the body.

Coach's corner: The distance between the two goals is essential in this drill. The drill must be challenging without being impossible. Make the goalies practice both sides of the body equally. I would advise keeping a pile of balls near each goal. This will prevent the goalies from having to get up to fetch the loose balls.

Alternatives to this drill: Practice the drill as designed.

Drill 2: Face the Shot

The goalie stands on the goal line and faces the inside of the goal. The coach or a second player passes or throws the ball toward the corners of the goal. The coach or player will call out "turn" when the ball is halfway to the goal. The goalie will have to turn and save the ball before it enters the goal. The throws can be high or low.

BACK IS TO THE THROWER

Setup: The player throwing the ball should be about 10 yards out from the goal line.

Key skills learned: This drill will dramatically increase the goalie's reaction time. The goalie will improve reflexes, hand-eye coordination and motor skills.

Coach's corner: Alter the throws to prevent the goalie from getting into a pattern. The more the goalie has to react to the ball, the more her body will learn to develop the movements in a quicker manner.

Alternatives to this drill: Practice the drill as designed.

Drill 3: Reaction

Four to six players line up about eight yards out from the goal. Each player has two balls in her possession. Players take turns throwing the balls at the goal. This can be accomplished by going down the line, or assigning numbers to the players and calling them at random to decide who throws the next ball. No matter which method you prefer, it is important to throw the balls in a rapid order. The goalie should just be able to regain balance before being forced to save the next throw. If the goalie is on the ground after a diving save, allow her to get up from the ground, but do not allow her to recover to the center position before the next ball is thrown.

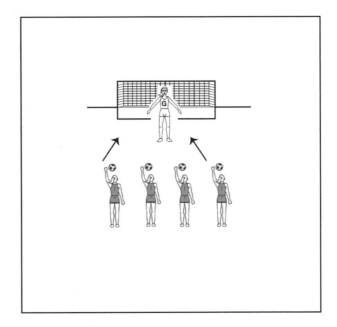

Setup: This drill can be completed with as many players and balls as desired by the coach.

Key skills learned: Goalies are forced to improve their reaction time in this drill. They also improve their ability to make saves from awkward positions.

Coach's corner: The timing or pace between throws is key to the success of this drill. The players throwing the balls should allow only enough time for the goalie to regain balance or recover to a standing position. Instruct the throwers that the idea is not to throw the ball past the goalie, but to force the goalie to make good saves.

Alternatives to this drill: Practice the drill as designed.

Drill 4: Over the Wall

Set up a wall of players about eight to 10 yards out from the goal line. Make sure the goalie cannot see clearly through the wall. The coach or a player throws the ball over the wall toward different areas of the goal. This will force the goalie to react quickly to make the save.

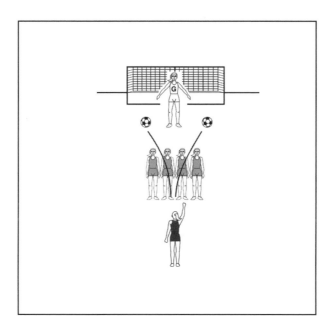

Setup: Set up drill as shown above.

Key skills learned: This is a representation of what the goalie faces in a direct or indirect kick situation. This drill forces the goalie to develop faster reflexes.

Coach's corner: Alter the throws to keep the goalie from getting into a pattern.

Alternatives to this drill: Practice the drill as designed.

Drill 5: Breakaway

This drill will help the goalie develop the ability to stop a breakaway attempt. The offensive player will take the ball down the center of the field and force the goalie to come off the goal line. The goalie will try to take away the offensive player's angle and make the save. The goalie cannot come out farther than the cones and the offensive player must shoot before the cones. This safety precaution is to prevent injuries while still practicing a real breakaway situation.

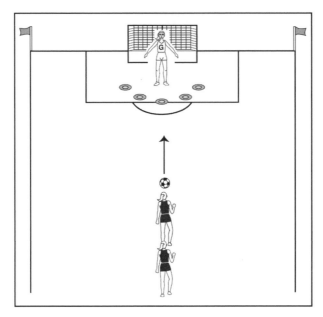

Setup: Coaches decide how far from the goal line they wish to place the protection cones.

Key skills learned: Goalies are put under the pressure of a one-on-one situation. The first thing the goalies will practice is when to come out of the goal. Goalies will also learn how close to the player they should come before going down to cover the lower angles. Finally, goalies will gain experience by seeing different styles of attacks from different offensive players.

Coach's corner: After each attempt, take the time to critique the goalie's actions. This drill may be your only opportunity to improve the goalie's ability to stop a one-on-one breakaway.

Alternatives to this drill: The safety zone is there to prevent injuries, but it also prevents offensive players from making moves around the goalie. The drill can be altered to allow this type of attack, but to prevent injuries, make sure the players back off the ball if the goalie is going to make contact with it.

Drill 6: Second-Six Safety

The goalie practices how to come out of the goal and grab crosses out of the air. Select four or five players to stand in the box and remain in their positions. Cross kicks are sent into the 18-yard box, and the goalie must come out of the goal and catch the ball at its highest point. Move the players around the box after a few crosses to keep the goalie focused.

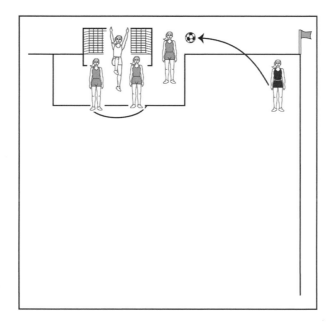

Setup: There needs to be space between the players so that the goalie has a lane in which to attack the ball.

Key skills learned: This drill will help the goalie develop confidence in coming out to catch crosses or to collect loose balls that are inside the 18-yard box.

Coach's corner: Start the drill with the token players in the box just standing still and being a hindrance to the goalie. As the goalie's skill and confidence grow, have the token players make runs, but not actually try to win the ball. The confusion caused by the movement of the players inside the box is more like the real situation the goalie will face in the games.

Alternatives to this drill: Teams can practice actual corner kick plays against the goalie. Instruct players not to attack the ball if the goalie calls for it.

Drill 7: Crossbar Touches

The goalie starts out on a line drawn about seven yards from the goal. A player tosses the ball to the crossbar of the goal. The goalie must retreat back the seven yards and parry the ball over the crossbar.

Setup: Cones should be set seven yards out from the goal line.

Key skills learned: The skill of pushing the ball over the top of the goal is not a commonly practiced, but it is very important that a goalie be able to perform it correctly.

Coach's corner: Not every throw will be a good one. Help the goalie decide when it is appropriate to parry the ball or simply catch it.

Alternatives to this drill: Change the drill by throwing some balls wide to the left or to the right to force the goalie to practice pushing the ball wide of the goal.

CHAPTER 5
OFFENSE

There are so many styles, beliefs, and systems on how to attack the opponent's goal that it would be impossible to cover them all. Instead I have picked several different drills that can be adapted to fit almost any offensive system.

Drill 1: Drop Shot

Player (2) passes the ball to the corner for player (1). Player (1) brings the ball into the box. The coach yells "drop" or "cross" and player (1) executes what has been asked. Player (2) or (3) finishes the drill with a shot on the goal.

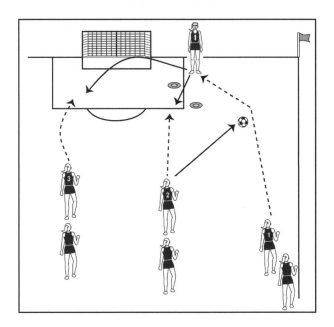

Setup/rotation: The two cones should be no more than seven yards off the end line. Rotate players so that (1) becomes (2), (2) becomes (3) and (3) becomes (1).

Key skills learned: This drill is designed to teach forwards and halfbacks the value of taking the space if it is given to them on the wings. The closer they can bring the ball to the goal, the better the opportunity they will have to make a good drop pass or cross. Players will also learn how to make the appropriate runs into the box and improve their ability to score from a crossed ball.

Coach's corner: Illustrate how important it is to challenge the fullbacks in this situation. If players can bring the ball in from the corner, the odds are in their favor to score. Too often players blindly take it to the corner and cross even if they are unmarked. By bringing the ball into the defense you are forcing them to come out of the mouth of the goal, and this makes passing lanes more available.

Alternatives to this drill: Practice the drill as designed.

Drill 2: Overlap "Through" Ball

Player (1) passes to a running player (2). Player (2) drops the ball in behind the defense (through the cones) to player (1). Player (1) then crosses the ball to the players waiting in line (2). The players in line (2) finish the drill with a shot on the goal.

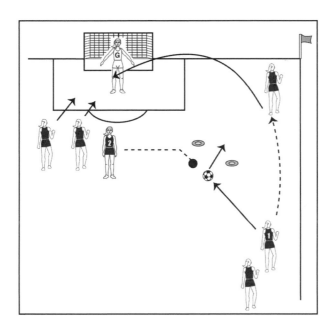

Setup/rotation: Line (2) should only consist of three to four players. Rotate players from (1) to (2). Player (1) is responsible for retrieving the soccer ball after the shot.

Key skills learned: Players learn to attack the defense by using a "through" ball. Being able to put the ball behind the defense where your player has a good chance of receiving it is instrumental in gaining scoring opportunities. Players waiting their turn in line (2) will also be able to practice finishing the ball from a cross.

Coach's corner: It is important to stress to the active players in line (2) that they must "show" or "go" to the ball. This is what creates the separation from the full-back and allows the pass from line (1). Remind the players waiting the cross in line (2) to be not inside the box before the ball arrives. Players must time their runs to meet the ball.

Alternatives to this drill: Practice the drill as designed.

Drill 3: Breakaway Advantage

The offense lines up five to 10 yards ahead of the defensive line. The coach throws or kicks the ball out in front of both lines. The first player in each line attempts to win the ball. Offense is given the edge to recreate the pressure of a breakaway situation. The defense must attempt to prevent the offensive player from scoring.

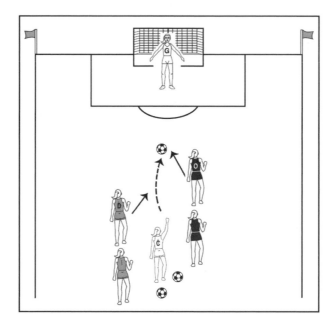

Rotation: You can have the players rotate lines if desired or leave the lines separated based on a player's position.

Key skills learned: This drill is for practicing one-on-one breakaway situations. The players need to learn to judge how much time they have before the defender can make a play at the ball. This drill also allows the offensive player to become familiar with the excitement of the moment and helps her prepare for this situation in the game. Dribbling with speed and finishing are the skills practiced in this drill.

Coach's corner: Monitor when the offensive player decides to take the shot. You want the player to get as close to the goal as possible without cutting down the angles and without being caught by the defense. The defensive player must practice the technique for forcing the player away from the goal.

Alternatives to this drill: You can vary the type of passes to the offensive player to include: on the ground, in the air, to the sides of the goal , etc.

Drill 4: Three-Man Advantage

Player (1) passes the ball to player (1a) who passes the ball back. Player (1) then plays the ball into space down the line. Player (2) times the run to arrive just behind the pass. Player (2) must then cross the ball to player (1a). Player (1a) finishes the drill with a shot on the goal.

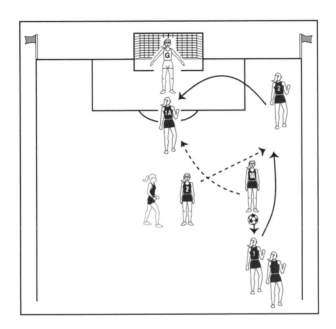

Setup/rotation: You may find it helpful to place a target cone where you want the pass to be received by player (2). Rotate players so that (1) becomes (1a), (1a) becomes (2) and (2) becomes (1).

Key skills learned: This drill teaches players the importance of playing the ball into space. It can also be used on the field as a plan to create space for the forwards. Players will practice short passing, crossing and finishing while performing this drill.

Example: Player (1) is the outside midfielder and player (1a) is the right forward. Imagine if you were attacking up the wing on this play. The fullback is guarding the right forward. When the forward comes to receive the pass, the fullback must come with the forward. That leaves the space behind the fullback open for the center half/forward to run into and receive the pass.

Coach's corner: It is important that the pass to player (2) is in front of the player and down the line. The idea of this drill is to get player (2) to run in behind the pass for a quick attack on the defense. You do not want player (2) to arrive before the pass and be forced to wait to receive the ball. Explain to the players that the ball does not always need to be played to a person. Sometimes it is easier for your teammate to run to the ball.

Alternatives to this drill: Player (1a) may be instructed to follow the play for a drop pass from player (2) instead of receiving a cross.

Drill 5: 18-Yard Play

Player (1) passes to player (2). Player (2) then drop passes to player (3). Player (3) crosses the ball to player (1) who finishes the drill with a shot on the goal.

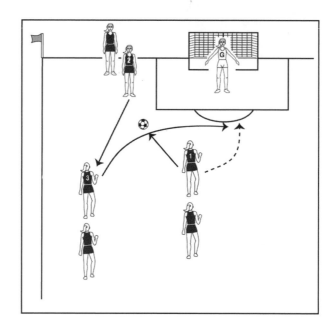

Rotation: Rotate players so that (1) becomes (2), (2) becomes (3) and (3) becomes (1).

Key skills learned: This drill simulates the game situation that often occurs around the 18-yard box of your opponent. Players will practice passing, crossing and finishing while performing this drill.

Coach's corner: All of the passes in this drill should be one-touch passes. Players do not have time in a game situation to take too many touches in this area of the field.

Alternatives to this drill: Practice the drill as designed.

Offense

Drill 6: Criss-Cross Score

Player (2) passes the ball through the cones to player (1). Player (1) then crosses the ball to the penalty spot. Players (2) and (3) make crossing runs to finish the cross from player (1).

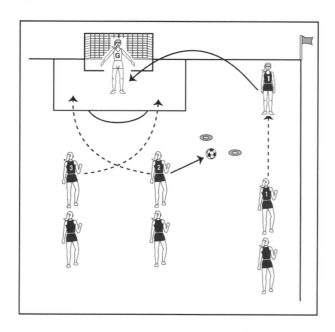

Setup/rotation: Two cones should be set up 10 yards from the 18-yard box as shown in the diagram above. Rotate players so that (1) becomes (2), (2) becomes (3) and (3) becomes (1).

Key skills learned: This drill is designed to help the offense practice a coordinated attack on the goal. The elements focused on in this particular drill are leading the forward with a pass, kicking a good cross, timing runs to receive a cross, and finishing the ball from a cross.

Coach's corner: The players who make the runs into the penalty box must time their runs to meet the ball while running forward. The runners do not want to be in the box before the cross, causing them to retreat backward to get the ball.

Alternatives to this drill: Practice the drill as designed.

Drill 7: Halfback Attack

Player (1) passes to a running player (2). Player (2) sends a long pass into the corner for player (3). Player (3) crosses the ball to players (1) and (2).

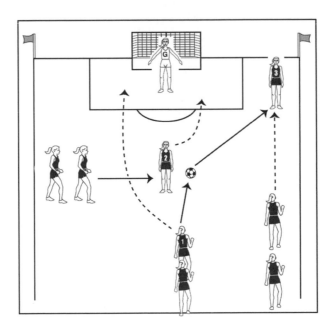

Rotation: Rotate players so that (1) bcomes (2), (2) becomes (3) and (3) becomes (1).

Key skills learned: This drill is specifically designed to simulate a game situation in which the halfbacks are starting the attack from the center of the field. Passing, crossing and finishing skills are practiced in this drill.

Coach's corner: Observe how well the players are timing their runs. Players (2) and (3) should not have to wait on the ball to arrive, they should be running to meet the passes. Player (3) should be even or a small distance ahead of player (2) when player (2) first receives the ball.

Alternatives to this drill: This drill can be run from the left or the right side of the field.

Drill 8: Inside-Out Offense

Player (1) passes the ball to player (2). Player (2) drop passes the ball back to player (1) who has moved to a supporting position. Player (1) then passes to player (3) as player (3) is running down the outside of the field. Player (3) crosses the ball to player (2) who finishes the drill with a shot on the goal.

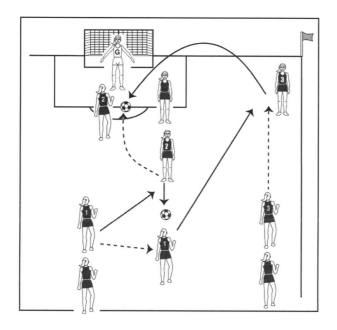

Setup/rotation: Players form three lines in a triangle formation. Lines (1) and (3) should be about 35 yards out from the goal. Line (2) should start with the last player in the line standing on the 18-yard box. Rotate players so that (1) becomes (2), (2) becomes (3) and (3) becomes (1).

Key skills learned: Players simulate attacking the goal. Short passing, moving to a supporting position, crossing and finishing are the skills practiced in this drill.

Coach's corner: Player (2) must move to receive the ball. Coming to the ball prevents defenders from intercepting the pass. Player (3) should begin to run when player (2) receives the ball.

Alternatives to this drill: Practice the drill as designed.

Drill 9: Throw-In

The first player in line (1) steps onto the field to become player (1a). Player (1a) starts the drill 15 yards away from the thrower. Player (1) throws the ball to player (1a) who is running to the ball. Player (1a) traps the ball and passes it back to player (1). Player (1) steps onto the field and crosses the ball in front of the goal to player (2). Player (2) finishes the drill with a shot on the goal.

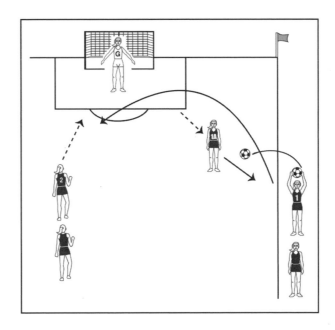

Setup/rotation: Position the players as diagramed above. Rotate so that (1) becomes (1a) and (1a) becomes (2).

Key skills learned: Players practice setting up a scoring opportunity from a throw-in. Players practice trapping, crossing and finishing while completing this drill.

Coach's corner: Instruct player (1a) to run to the thrower. In a game situation the player must "show" to the ball or they will not be open to receive the throw. If the players are capable, see whether can one-touch the pass back to player (1). This can be done with their feet, head, or chest.

Alternatives to this drill: Move line (2) to the center of the field. Instead of having player (1a) trap the ball, have player (1a) slip-head the ball to a running player (2). Player (2) then finishes with a shot on the goal.

Drill 10: Give and Go

Player (1) passes the ball to player (1a). Player (1a) passes the ball back to player (1) and makes a run to the corner. Player (1) chips the pass into the space ahead of player (1a). Player (1a) crosses the ball to a running player (2). Player (2) then finishes this drill with a shot on the goal.

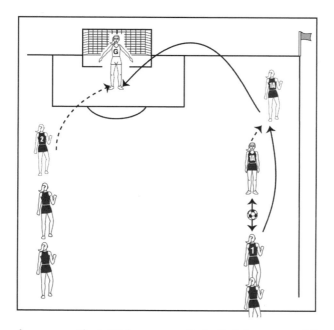

Rotation: Rotate players so that (1) becomes (1a), (1a) becomes (2) and (2) becomes (1).

Key skills learned: This drill is for practicing a two-player attack down the wing. The players must practice coming to receive the pass, making a good drop pass, chipping the ball at the proper distance, and striking a good cross.

Coach's corner: Player (1a) must come to receive the pass. If the player does not move forward in a game situation, then a fullback will step into the passing lane and steal the ball.

Alternatives to this drill: Practice the drill from the right or left side of the field.

Drill 11: Overlap Attack

Player (3) shows to the ball and receives a pass from player (1). Player (2) makes an overlapping run and receives a pass from player (3). Player (2) then crosses the ball over line (3) to player (1) who finishes with a shot on the goal.

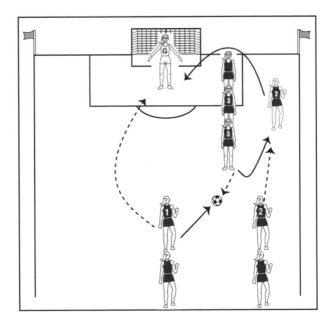

Setup/rotation: Make sure line (3) is located as shown in the diagram. Rotate players so that (1) becomes (3), (3) becomes (2) and (2) becomes (1).

Key skills learned: Players learn to make overlapping runs in this drill based on a forward/midfielder situation. They will also practice the skills of lead passing, crossing and finishing.

Coach's corner: Use line (3) as a wall for player (2) to cross the ball over. Remind everyone to pay attention during this drill to avoid being hit by a bad cross. It is key that player (3) passes the ball in front of player (2) so that player (2) can run to the ball.

Alternatives to this drill: Practice the drill as designed.

Drill 12: Chip and Charge

Three lines form a triangle about 10 to 15 yards apart from each other. Player (1) passes to player (2). Player (2) drop passes to player (3) who then chips the ball over line (2) for a running player (1). Player (1) finishes the drill with a shot on the goal.

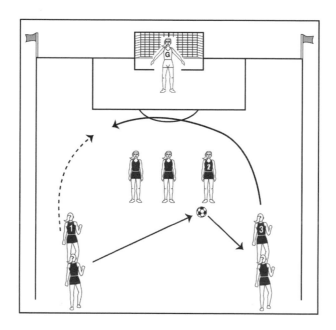

Setup/rotation: Make sure the lines are far enough away from the goal so that player (1) does not receive the chip pass too close to the goal. Player (1) should have time to control the pass, take one or two dribbles, and shoot the ball from around the corner of the 18-yard box. Rotate the players so that (1) becomes (2), (2) becomes (3) and (3) becomes (1).

Key skills learned: This drill teaches forwards and halfbacks a way to set up an attacking situation from half field. Players must practice coming to the ball, making a good chip pass to the open player, and finishing with a shot on the goal.

Coach's corner: Pay close attention to how quickly the player in line (3) plays the ball. This must be a one-touch pass or the player making the run in line (1) will be offside. Timing the run from line (1) is also very critical in this drill. If the player in line (1) goes too soon, she may be forced to wait on the pass from player (3).

Alternatives to this drill: This drill can be easily switched from right to left by moving the direction of the players waiting in line (2) and having the original pass come from the player in line (3).

Drill 13: Step-Over to Line

Player (1) passes the ball through the cones to player (2). Player (2) performs the through-the-legs step-over move and takes the ball down the line. Player (2) can either drop pass or cross the ball to player (1).

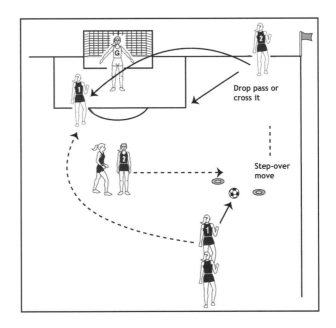

Setup/rotation: The two cones should be set up 12 yards out from the 18-yard box. Rotate the players so that (1) becomes (2) and (2) becomes (1). Player (1) is responsible for retrieving the soccer ball after the shot.

Key skills learned: This drill helps to improve the speed at which the player can receive the ball, turn and attack the defense. This ability is especially useful to outside forwards and midfielders.

Coach's corner: Player (2) should not have to wait to receive the ball. The players need to pass the ball to the open space before the player has reached the desired reception location. The "through-the-legs step-over move" can be found on page 18.

Alternatives to this drill: Player (1) may be instructed to follow the play for a drop pass from player (2) instead of receiving a cross.

CHAPTER 6
OFFENSE VS. DEFENSE

The ability to monitor both offensive and defensive techniques in the same drill makes this chapter key in the development of any team.

Drill 1: Three on Two to Goal

The defense lines up on both sides of the goal and sends a long pass out to the offensive players. The offense attacks the goal with a three-to-two advantage. The defense must work as a team to defend against the attack and the offense must work together to get the best scoring opportunity.

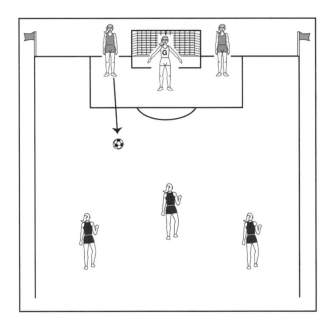

Setup: The defense will line up next to the goal posts and the offense should begin the drill 10 yards inside the half line.

Key skills learned: Offensive players will practice dribbling to beat an opponent, passing to a player or to space, and finishing. The defense will practice defensive positioning, jockeying and tackling the ball. This drill will also expose the defensive players to several different types of attacks they must learn to defend against.

Coach's corner: The offensive players begin the drill in a three-line system. Coaches need to make sure the offensive players do not just attack every time with left, right and center players. Coaches need to show the offense how to overlap runs and switch the direction of the attack. The defensive players must communicate and work as a team if they are going to stop the attack. Show them players how to eliminate the third offensive player by forcing the offense to use only one side of the field. Do not be afraid to stop the drill at any time and correct a missed opportunity or a bad position taken by the defense. This drill provides the coach with several different opportunities to show how to attack or defend in many different situations.

Alternatives to this drill: Coaches can choose the number of offensive and defensive players.

Drill 2: Half-Field Offense vs. Defense

Inside one half of the field the offense will scrimmage the defense. The offense will attack the goal and the defense will earn points by gaining possession of the ball and passing it through the goals located at the half line. The defensive goals will symbolize the ability of the defense to get the ball to the outside halfbacks.

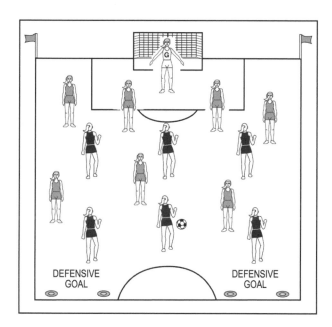

Setup: Two defensive goals need to be marked with cones on the half line as shown in the diagram above.

Key skills learned: Playing together as a unit is the skill most practiced during this drill. Both the offense and the defense must learn to play together to be successful on the field. The offense can practice whichever method of attack desired by the coach and the defense can learn to defend as a unit.

Coach's corner: The key to this drill is the placement of the halfbacks. If the objective of the drill is to focus on the attack, then put your starting halfbacks as offense. Switch the starting halfbacks to defense if the goal is to work with the defensive players on how to clear the ball out of their own team's half.

Alternatives to this drill: Practice the drill as designed.

Drill 3: The Quest

This drill consists of three different sections of two-on-one. The defense cannot come off the back line of each grid until the offense enters that individual grid. The offense must pass or dribble around the defender without leaving the boundary of the grid. The defense must stop pursuing the offense if the ball crosses the back line of her grid. The next defender can come off of the back line as soon as the ball crosses into her grid. The offense must make it past all three grids before they can finish with a shot on the goal.

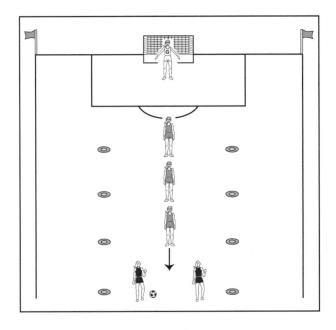

Setup/rotation: Three grids are marked with cones. The grids are 10 yards wide and long to form three squares in a row. The defense must line up at the back of each square. Rotate by switching out the defensive players after a set amount of time.

Key skills learned: Offensive players will have to work together in order to beat all three defenders in a row. This drill will teach players how to pass and move in a small area. Players will also have to use dribbling skills and strategies in order to complete this drill.

Coach's corner: Advise the offensive players that they must move in all directions and cannot simply have one player left and one player right. Show them the advantage created if the player without the ball runs to an open position behind the defender.

Instruct the defense that if a loose ball comes into their grid, they need to attack it immediately. This will help them realize that in game situations there are times when their need to leave their mark, if they can win the ball.

Alternatives to this drill: Practice the drill as designed.

Drill 4: Defensive Positioning

Two offensive players dribble and pass the ball to each other while the defender practices the appropriate position in which to defend. The defender does not try to take the ball from the offense and the offense does not try to get past the defense until the latter crosses the line set up by the cones. At this point in the drill, the two on one is real and the offensive players try to score a goal against the defensive player.

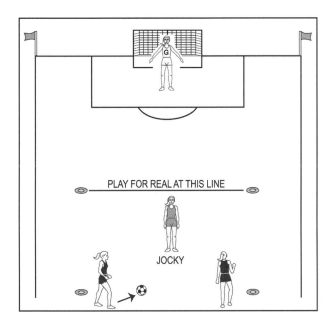

Setup: The "start play line" is set up 12 yards out from the 18-yard box. The width of the "jockey" part of the drill should be only 12 yards apart. The length of this section can be determined by the coach.

Key skills learned: The defense will learn how to adjust to the changing position of the ball and how it affects the defensive position. The offense will learn patience in attacking in a two-on-one situation.

Coach's corner: The offensive players must stay within the 12-yard wide area. This will allow the defensive player to see both offensive players at the same time. Stop the drill if the she is not taking the right position and explain where the defense needs to be and why. Instruct the offense to move slowly to allow the defender to adjust to the ball. The idea of this drill is to teach the defender the appropriate positioning. If the offense sprints through the first part of the drill, the defender does not get the necessary practice.

Alternatives to this drill: Practice the drill as designed.

Drill 5: Team Possession

Two teams with an equal number of players try to maintain possession of the ball inside a small area. The players may pass or dribble the ball. The objective is to see how many passes can be completed before the other team steals the ball. If the other team manages to steal the ball, it must now play keep-away from the first team. Coaches should set a goal number of passes to be completed.

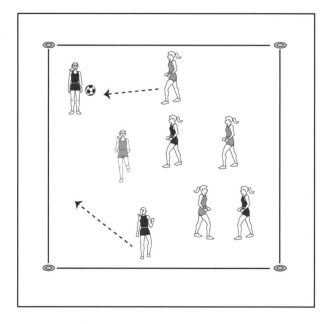

Setup: This drill can be completed inside the 18-yard box, center circle, or any size area that the coach outlines with cones.

Key skills learned: Players will practice how to make good passes inside a small area. Players will also practice getting open for a pass, dribbling the ball through other players, and playing as a team.

Coach's corner: The teams need to be even in skill. If one team is far stronger than the other team, then the weaker team will rarely be able to practice offense. During the play, point out where the open space is located so that players on both teams can learn to look and find it on their own. Players may not even notice the open area if it is not brought to their attention.

Alternatives to this drill: Make it a contest between the two teams. The team that makes seven complete passes wins the game and the losing team must do some physical work; for example, push-ups, sit-ups or sprints.

Drill 6: Line Soccer

Teams of four or five players compete in a small-sized scrimmage. Teams can score by dribbling the ball across the opposing team's end line. The players who score must have complete control over the ball or it is turned over to the defensive team. Regular soccer rules apply, except that no player can be offside.

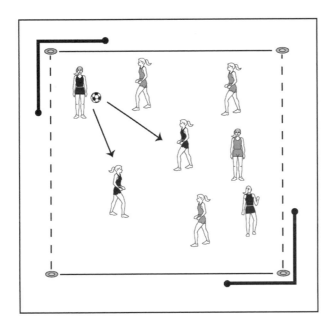

Setup: The size of the grid should depend on the number of players completing the drill and their skill level.

Key skills learned: Small-sized scrimmages are great practice for many of the skills needed to be successful at soccer. Offensive players must be able to maintain possession of the ball, dribble to beat an opponent, make good passes, move into space, and receive the ball with skill. Defensively, players must mark up, set up a good defensive stance, communicate with their teammates, cover the pressure defender, and disrupt the offense by stealing passes or dispossessing the ball handler.

Coach's corner: Communication on both sides of the field is crucial in small-sized games. If players don't help each other immediately, they will lose possession to the other team. Instruct players to make checking runs to the ball. In a limited amount of space, players cannot expect to stand still to receive a pass. Inform the offense to make sure there is always one player back in case of a counter attack.

Alternatives to this drill: Small goals may be added to the field. A coach may also choose to allow the teams to score on either the end line or a side line. This splits the field in an angle with each team defending two lines. This v-shaped goal promotes switching the direction of play.

Drill 7: Four Square Possession

The offense is broken up into four squares of equal numbers of offensive play-ers. The defense will have fewer players than the offense but will be able to move from square to square. The offense can pass from square to square but the players must not move outside of their assigned square. The offense attempts to keep pos-session of the ball by passing and dribbling around the defense.

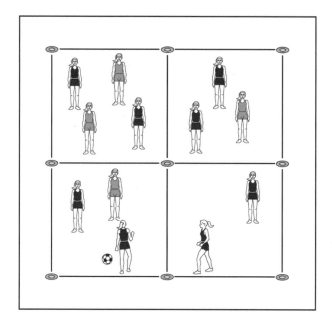

Setup: The size of the squares should be even and should reflect how many players you have assigned to each square. Players need to be able to move five to 10 yards apart.

Key skills learned: This drill is designed to help players maintain possession of the ball in a small area. This drill also shows players the benefit of finding the open player away from the congested areas of the field. Passing, dribbling and switch-ing the field are the skills learned by the offense in this drill. Defensively, play-ers learn to work as a unit, limit the amount of space in which the offense has to maneuver, and intercept passes.

Coach's corner: Before your team attempts this drill, make sure your players have the ability to play five-on-two with relative skill. The goal of the offense is to move the ball from corner to corner to spread out the defense. The defense needs to work together to trap the offensive players in one area of the field.

Alternatives to this drill: Practice the drill as designed.

Drill 8: Wide Zone Scrimmage

Two teams play a controlled scrimmage with the outside forwards being confined to a wide zone. The forwards cannot leave this zone and the defense cannot enter. Teams play by soccer's regular rules but there are no offsides. Teams are encouraged to get the ball to the forwards so they can cross it, but if the defense gives them an open shot in the center of the field, the players should take it.

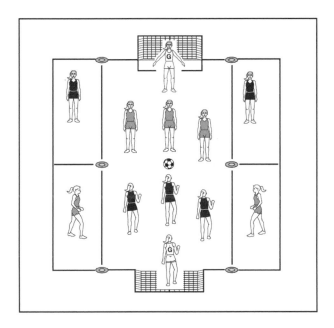

Setup: This drill works best with 12 or 14 players. The field should be no more than 40 yards long and wide. The forward's zone should start at the half line and be at least 10 yards out from the nearest goal post.

Key skills learned: The players will learn the advantages of getting the ball to the outside of the field. The players will also practice crossing and finishing in front of the goal.

Coach's corner: Goals can be scored by going straight up the middle, but encourage the players to use the outside forwards whenever possible. The forwards cannot lose possession and they give each team the best opportunity to score by crossing, drop passing and shooting the ball directly. You may wish to award more points for goals that are scored from a cross.

Alternatives to this drill: Allow the defense to enter the forwards' zones. Continue to the next page for an alternative to this drill.

Drill 9: Wide Zone Neutral

This is an alternative to the drill listed on the previous page. This drill has neutral players that are restricted to playing only inside the grids. They play for whichever team passes them the ball. The objective is to get the ball wide to the neutral players who then cross the ball in front of the goal. All goals must be scored from a cross.

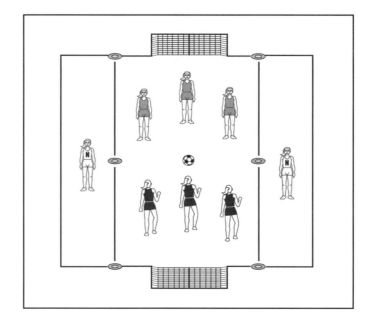

Setup/rotation: The field is no more than 40 yards long and wide. The outside zones should start at least 10 yards out from the goal posts. Rotate the neutral players after a set amount of time.

Key skills learned: This drill focuses on crossing the ball and finishing from a crossed ball. Players will also learn to get the ball out wide to the outside midfielders or forwards.

Coach's corner: Designate the players you feel would most likely be crossing the balls in the game to be the neutral players. This drill gives them the opportunity to practice without the pressure of the defense. Instruct the neutral players to set up the cross by cutting the ball at an angle toward the center of the field before striking the cross. This will help the player to make a more accurate pass.

Alternatives to this drill: Coaches can make a rule that all players on the team must touch the ball before that team can score. Coaches may also designate that all scoring must be from a header. Goalkeepers can be added to the game when a coach feels the team is ready to progress to that level.

Offense vs. Defense

Drill 10: Out from the Back

The offense tries to keep the defense from successfully clearing the ball out of the defensive zone. Six defensive players will try and work the ball out of the back against only four offensive players. This drill starts with the center forward being marked inside the half by the stopper. Three other offensive players are lined up at half field. The center player sends the ball deep to the left or the right of the field, andoffensive and defensive players race each other to the ball. (The drill is set up so that the defense should get to the ball first.) The defensive players must then pass or dribble the ball until they are able to cross the half line with the ball.

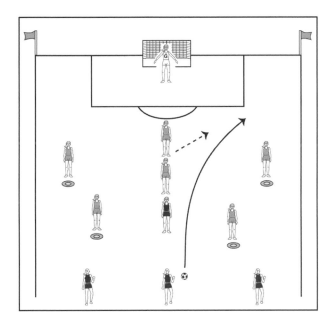

Setup: The left and right fullbacks and midfielders are lined up at the cones to start the drill. The stopper marks the center forward. Three other offensive players start the drill from the half line.

Key skills learned: This drill will help teach the defense how to gain control of the ball and effectively pass it out to the offense. The offensive players will practice how to trap the defense in their own half and force a turnover.

Coach's corner:

Offense: Before the drill begins, explain to each player the position she is trying to get to when this situation occurs in the game. Teach the players the style or system you prefer in trapping the defense in its own zone.

Defense: Walk through what will happen when the ball is kicked deep. Show them how the offensive midfielders will follow the forward in support of the ball. Instruct the defensive players on how you want them to work the ball out of the defensive zone.

Alternatives to this drill: Practice the drill as designed.

CHAPTER 7
MULTIPLE DRILLS IN A SET FORMATION

This chapter contains drills that cover a wide variety of skills without changing the configuration of the practice area. These drills are perfect if space and time are factors in how you practice.

Drill 1: Technical Grid (Passing)

Four players at the corners of a grid deliver passes to a player in the center. The player in the center returns the pass back to the original passer. To keep from just going around in a circle, the players on the outside determine who passes the ball by calling the center player's name. The center player must not control who passes the ball next, but instead listens for her name to be called.

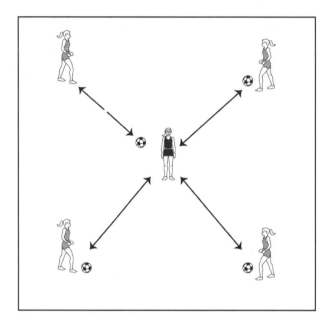

Setup/rotation: Passers should be 10 yards from the center of the grid. Rotate the center player after a set amount of time.

Key skills learned: Players practice making short one-touch passes while completing this drill. They are able to get many touches on the ball in a short amount of time. The players must concentrate and perform the task even as their bodies get tired.

Coach's corner: Make sure that the players stay on their toes and are forced to react to the ball. Monitor the passes. They need to stay on the ground and be struck with the appropriate pace. Have the player in the middle retreat back to the center of the grid after each pass.

Alternatives to this drill: Coaches may wish to have two players in the center completing the drill simultaneously. Continue to the next page.

Drill 2: Technical Grid (Trapping)

The players on the outside toss the ball to the center player. The player in the center practices controlling the ball with different body parts and passing the ball back to the thrower. The players should alternate who tosses the ball by calling the person in the center by name.

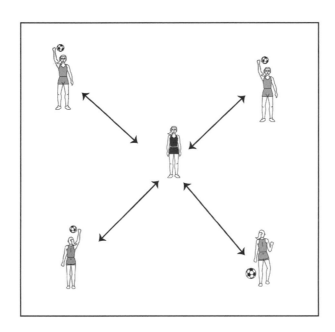

Setup/rotation: Passers should be 10 yards from the center of the grid. Rotate the center player after a set amount of time.

Key skills learned: Fundamental trapping and passing skills are practiced during this drill.

Coach's corner: Forcing the center player to move to the person calling her name is a good way to keep the player from standing on her heels while trapping the ball. Monitor the players to ensure that proper techniques are being used to control the ball. Alternate throws to different body parts to keep the players from becoming complacent.

Alternatives to this drill: Coaches may wish to have two players in the center completing the drill simultaneously. Continue to the next page.

Drill 3: Technical Grid (Heading)

The players on the outside toss the ball to the center player. The player in the center practices heading the ball back to the thrower. The players should alternate who tosses the ball by calling the person in the center by name.

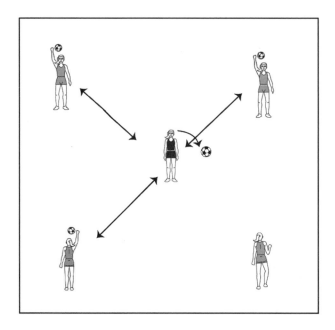

Setup/rotation: Passers should be 10 yards from the center of the grid. Rotate the center player after a set amount of time.

Key skills learned: This drill is great for practicing heading the ball to a target area.

Coach's corner: Make sure the center player keeps her eyes open and follows through with her head toward the target. Do not let the player stop forward movement after the ball makes contact. The headers should be aimed back at the thrower's chest.

Alternatives to this drill: Coaches may wish to have two players in the center completing the drill simultaneously. Continue to the next page.

Drill 4: Technical Grid (Offense vs. Defense)

There are four players on the outside, but only three have soccer balls. Inside the grid there is an offensive and defensive player. The outside players pass the ball to the offensive player who must find the open player (without a ball) and make a pass to her. The offensive player is not allowed to pass the ball back to the original passer. The defensive player must try to keep the offensive player from completing the pass to the open player.

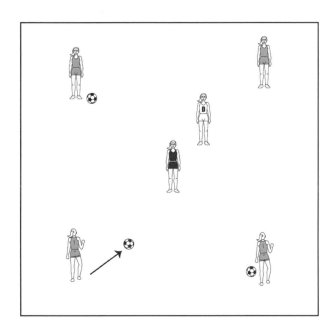

Setup/rotation: Passers should be 10 yards from the center of the grid. Switch the offensive and defensive players after a set amount of time. When both center players have competed in both roles, bring in two new players.

Key skills learned: Players must shield the ball, find the open player, and get the ball to the open player by beating the defender in a limited amount of space.

Coach's corner: The outside players need to communicate to the center offensive player by informing her of where the open player can be located. Make sure the offensive player keeps the ball on the opposite side of the body from where the defender is located. Dribble with the left foot if the defender is on the right and vice versa.

Alternatives to this drill: Practice the drill as designed.

Drill 5: Line Skills (Passing)

Three players line up 10 yards from each other with each outside player having a soccer ball. The center player receives alternating passes from both partners. The center player plays left and then turns to receive the pass from the player on the right. The outside players should time their passes so that the player in the center has little time to react to the pass.

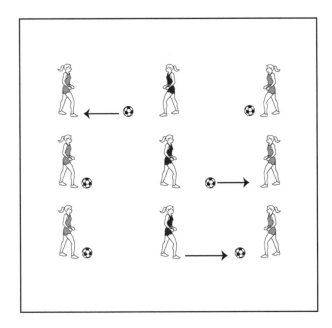

Rotation: The center player rotates out after a set amount of time.

Key skills learned: This drill is great for short passing. Being able to locate the ball quickly and to make a good pass are the skills practiced in this drill.

Coach's corner: Make sure the players stay on their toes and are constantly looking for the next pass. The players on the outside must pass the ball as the center player is turning to receive it.

Alternatives to this drill: Continue to the next page.

Drill 6: Line Skills (Trapping)

Three players line up 10 yards from each other with the outside players each having a soccer ball. The center player receives tosses from both partners. The center player must trap the ball and pass it back to the thrower. The center player plays left and then turns to receive the toss from the player on the right. The outside players should time their throws so that the player in the center has little time to react to the toss.

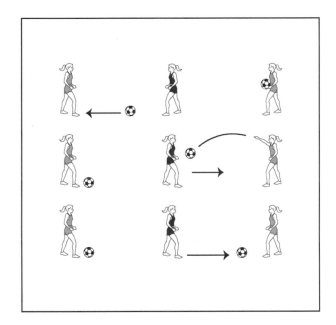

Rotation: The center player rotates out after a set amount of time.

Key skills learned: Players must concentrate in order to keep the ball under control. They learn to complete this drill under the pressure that the next toss is already coming. This helps them perform the task better in a game situation.

Coach's corner: Make sure the players stay on their toes and are constantly looking for the next toss. However, do not let them sacrifice good technique just because they are expecting the next ball. Being able to control the ball under pressure is essential to being a good player. Use all body parts for this drill.

Alternatives to this drill: You can also practice heading the ball in this manner. Continue to the next page.

Drill 7: Line Skills (Quick Turn)

The player in the center practices the "quick-turn move". The player runs to the pass, performs the quick-turn move and passes to the other outside player. This process is repeated from both sides.

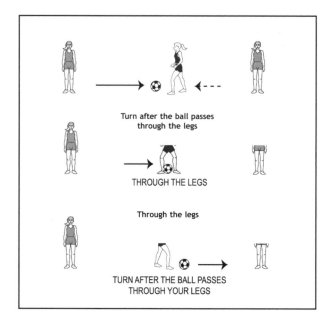

Setup/rotation: The outside players should be 15 yards away from the center player. The center player rotates out after a set amount of time.

Key skills learned: This drill provides extensive practice of the quick-turn move. Players can improve their ability to receive the ball in one direction and quickly turn it to the opposite direction.

Coach's corner: The inside of the foot will automatically redirect the ball at the appropriate angle. Watch to make sure the players are not trying to swing their foot at the ball as it is rolling through their legs.

Alternatives to this drill: Continue to the next page.

Drill 8: Quick-Turn Move

Ball approaches.

Ball passes through the legs, but with a slight touch from the inside of the right foot.

Pivot turn on the left foot.

Face the other direction with the ball at the feet.

The player runs to the ball and lets it pass through her legs, slightly redirecting it with the inside of one foot, and turns quickly to face the other direction with the ball at her feet. The redirection not only places the ball where the next touch will be, but can also be used to slow the pace of the ball.

Drill 9: Line Skills (Volley)

Three players line up 10 yards from each other and each outside player has a ball. The center player receives tosses from both partners. The player in the center practices volleying the ball back to the thrower. The center player plays left and then turns to receive the toss from the player on the right. The outside players should time their throws so that the player in the center has little time to react to the toss. The center player should aim her volley at the thrower's chest.

Rotation: The center player rotates out after a set amount of time.

Key skills learned: This drill is great for the players to practice the contact, aim, and control of their volleys.

Coach's corner: The players should aim their volleys at the server's chest. Make sure the players are following through correctly. Players don't seem to follow through if they are not hitting the ball at full strength. If possible, the outside players should have extra balls at their feet to keep the drill going if the center player hits a volley that goes out of reach.

Alternatives to this drill: Continue to the next page.

Drill 10: Line skills (Slip-Headers)

Remove one ball and have the center player receive tosses from the outside players. The center player must slip head the ball behind her to the other partner. The center player plays left and then turns to receive the toss from the player on the right.

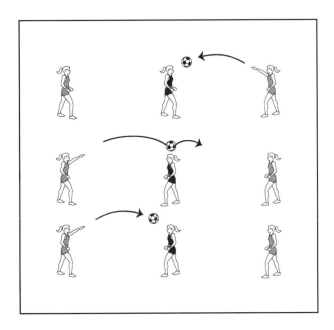

Rotation: The center player rotates out after a set amount of time.

Key skills learned: This drill is great for the players to practice the skill of slip heading the ball.

Coach's corner: The players must keep their eyes on the ball. Players cannot slip-head the ball if they cannot see it. Make sure the players bend at the knees to get a lower center of gravity. This also allows them to push up upon contact and increase the distance the ball travels.

Alternatives to this drill: Practice the drill as designed.

Drill 11: Four Corners (Passing)

Four cones are set in a square about 10 yards apart from each other. Equal numbers of players line up at the four cones. Passes can either go left or right depending on which foot you want this drill to target. Players begin the drill by having two balls at opposite corners of the square. In the example below, players are passing to the right. You can have the players pass and follow it to the next cone, or have the players pass to the right and run to the left or vice versa.

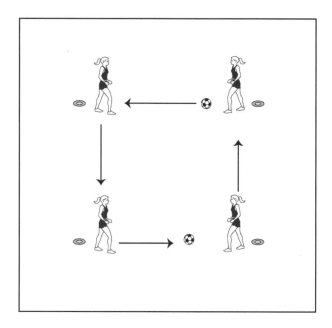

Setup: A minimum of eight players is needed to complete this drill.

Key skills learned: This drill is designed to make the players think as well as practice to improve their individual passing ability.

Coach's corner: This is a simple drill to perform; however, by changing the rules (see alternatives below) you can help players learn to think while playing soccer. Soccer is just as much a mental game as it is a physical one.

Alternatives to this drill: Change the rules of the drill to keep players mentally in the game. Examples:

      1. Pass right/left and follow the pass to the next line.

      2. Pass right and run left or vice versa.

      3. Play with three or four balls.

Continue to the next page.

Drill 12: Four Corners (Trapping)

Players toss the ball to the next player in a clockwise or counterclockwise manner. The players receiving the toss trap the ball in the direction of their next pass and not just in front of themselves. When the ball is under control, they complete the pass to the next player. Tosses can be to any of the body parts. Every other player will be tossing the ball to the next player.

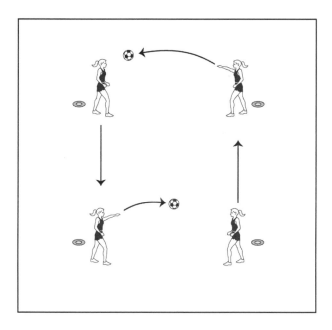

Rotation: Players rotate in a clockwise or counterclockwise direction.

Key skills learned: This drill is designed to make the players practice controlling the ball away from the defense.

Coach's corner: If a defender is on a player's right side the player will want to bring the ball down to the left side of her body. This will give the player time to shield the ball from the defender. Monitor the player to make sure she does not just trap the ball and turn once the ball is on the ground. The player's first touch should direct the ball to the desired side.

Alternatives to this drill: Players can toss the ball to the right or to the left. Coaches can also move back the cones based on the players' skill level. Also, instead of just tossing the ball the players can practice actual throw-ins.

CHAPTER 8
TEAM RELAY DRILLS

These drills are perfect for bringing competition into the practice. Players will give more effort and play at a higher work rate if they are grouped together to achieve a common goal.

Drill 1: Speed-Dribble Relay

Two teams race against each other to be the first to complete the relay. The first stage of the relay is an agility run. Players must face forward and step sideways left and right. The players will then dribble around the cones in a controlled-dribble exercise. After completing the second stage, the players must dribble to the far cone and make three complete circles around it while dribbling the ball. The players then return through the controlled-dribbling stage, leaving the ball at the start of the cones for the next player, and sidestepping through the last stage. The second player in the line may begin when the first player crosses the starting line.

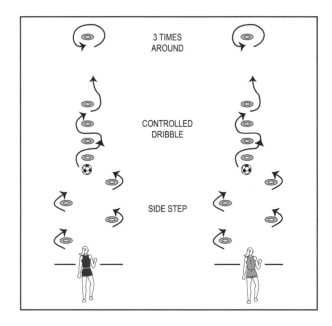

Setup: The coach can decide how far apart to set up the cones based on the skill level of the players completing the relay.

Key skills learned: Individual dribbling skills and team-building activities are the main focus of this relay.

Coach's corner: If a player misses a cone on the controlled-dribbling section, then she must return to the missed cone and correctly go around it. This may cost the player a lot of time, but it rewards those who take the time to complete the section correctly. Speed and skill are equal components in this relay and in the sport of soccer. Players also need to be aware of where they leave the ball for the next player in line. Stopping the ball correctly at the beginning of the controlled-dribbling section will save time for the next player completing the relay.

Alternatives to this drill: Coaches may change the number of cones in sections (1) or (2) to either increase or decrease the size of the relay. Coaches may also wish to replace the far cone with a big circle of cones. Players would then need to speed dribble around the circle before coming back through the second stage.

Drill 2: Team One-on-One

Two teams compete at the same time through an identical course. The first section is a controlled-dribbling exercise. When the player has dribbled past the last cone, she must go one-on-one with a defensive player provided by the other team. The defensive player must start the drill on the goal line. The offensive player must beat the defensive player by dribbling the ball over the line behind the defensive player and stopping the ball before it passes the back cone. If the defensive player takes the ball, kicks the ball out of the selected playing area, or the offensive player crosses the goal line but cannot stop the ball before the cone, then the offensive player must go to the back of the starting line and re-attempt the relay. If a player is stopped three times consecutively then that player gets a free pass behind the defensive player.

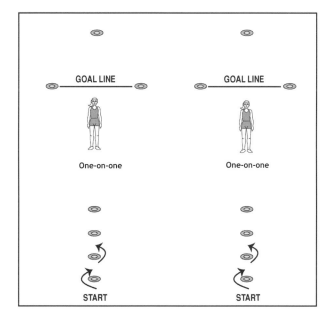

Setup: The distance between the last cone of the controlled-dribbling section and the goal line should be at least 12 yards.

Key skills learned: This is a team-building exercise that focuses on improving individual dribbling skills.

Coach's corner: Change the designated defender after each round and play the best of three or five rounds to give each team a fair chance to win the relay. This will prevent a team from winning simply because it happens to have the best defender in its group. Defenders must retreat back to the goal line after each individual player. The defense is not allowed to stand and wait at the end of the controlled-dribbling section.

Alternatives to this relay: To make the game more challenging, allow players to cross the goal line in either their grid or the other team's grid. Allowing them to use the whole field will spread out the defense and give the dribblers a better chance to cross the line.

Drill 3: Head-to-Head Dribbling

Two teams compete at the same time on the same course. The first section is side-by-side controlled dribbling. The first player through these obstacles can take the inside lead position. If a cone is missed, the player must go back to the missed cone and correctly go around it. The second section is cut dribbling. Players must cut the ball at an angle to be able to dribble to the next cone. This section is where most players will get passed by the other team because of mis-touching the ball and missing a cone. The third section is the speed dribble. Players must dribble with pace before reaching the final stage. The final stage is a take over or pass to the next player on their team.

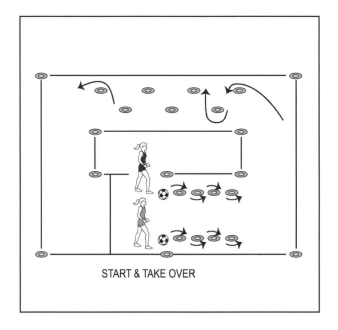

START & TAKE OVER

Setup: Coaches can choose the size of the relay area.

Key skills learned: This is a team-building exercise that forces the players to become more efficient at dribbling the soccer ball in several different manners.

Coach's corner: You will have to enforce the rules during this relay. If a player misses a cone, she will have to go back and correctly negotiate that cone before continuing forward.

Alternatives to this game: Complete the relay as designed.

Drill 4: One-on-One Relay

Two teams compete against each other to see which team can complete the drill with the most points. One player from each team will race the other through the cones. Players must step sideways left and right through the first section. The first player to the ball is offense and the second player must prevent the offensive player from scoring a goal. If the defender is able to take the ball, then the roles are switched. Teams score points by shooting the ball into the net. A shot that goes into the corner area is worth two points, while a shot down the center is only worth one point. If the ball is kicked out of bounds, then no points are awarded. The next player on each team may begin the relay when one of the players who went before her touches the ball. There may be many one-on-one drills going on at the same time.

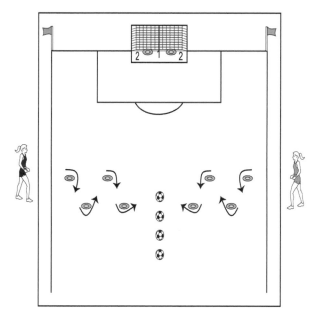

Setup: The running course should be set up 15 yards out from the 18- yard box.

Key skills learned: The player's fitness, agility and one-on-one skills are practiced in this relay.

Coach's corner: Coaches will have to keep score and determine the size of the playing area. Coaches may even place cones to outline the area in which a one on one can be played. If the ball leaves this area, then no points are awarded to either team.

Alternatives to this game: Complete the relay as designed.

Drill 5: Team Dribbling Relay

Two teams compete in a relay for the faster time. The first player must side - step left and right through the first section. The player must then dribble all the balls one by one to the other side of section (2). The third section is a controlled-dribbling section that ends with a player picking up a cone and returning through the controlled-dribbling section again. The other should leave the ball at the start of the controlled-dribbling section and sprint back to the line. Players do not have to go through section (1)or (2) again. The second player on the team can go when the player before her crosses the start line with the cone in her hand.

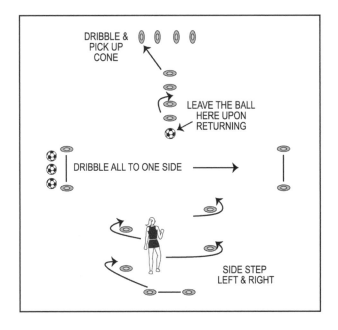

Setup: Construct the relay as designed.

Key skills learned: This relay helps the players work on their conditioning and dribbling skills. Players must race against the clock and each other while maintaining control of the ball.

Coach's corner: Coaches will have to keep the time and enforce the rules of the relay.

Alternatives to this game: Instead of competing against the clock, the coach may wish to have two identical courses set up side by side. Coaches may also have the players complete all the sections on the return trip.

CHAPTER 9
SKILL-BASED GAMES

We cannot forget that athletes play soccer because it is fun. Games are the best way to keep athletes interested during practice. Just because it is called a game does not mean the players cannot benefit from playing it. The games in this chapter will not only keep practice enjoyable, but will teach players necessary skills to better themselves individually and as a team.

Drill 1: Police

This game is played like Cops and Robbers. There are two or three cops that chase around the other players. If the cop steals a player's ball or kicks it outside the 18-yard box, then that player must go to jail (inside the six-yard box) with her ball. Players may be released from the six-yard box by being handed a "key" (a cone) from another player. Players may carry the keys with them, but if a cop steals their ball or kicks their ball out of the 18-yard box, then the players must drop the key where they lost possession of the ball. Cops cannot pick up the keys and players may only hand keys to the players in the jail. No one is allowed in the jail except those players who have been caught. The cops win the game when everyone is in jail.

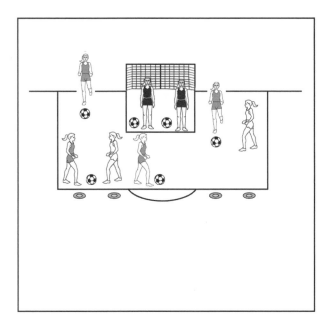

Setup: The 18-yard box is used as the field, and the total number of players should determine how many cops are used in the game. Place the keys on the 18-yard box to start the game.

Key skills learned: This game forces players to concentrate on their dribbling skills. Players must be able to avoid the cops by locating the open space, maintaining possession of their ball, and keeping their heads up while dribbling.

Coach's corner: The coach needs to be a judge in this game to make sure players are not handing off cones illegally and escaping from the six-yard box without a key. Players may not hand keys back and forth outside of the six-yard box to release all the players. A released player must dribble around the 18-yard box for 30 seconds before releasing another player.

Alternatives to this game: Play this game as designed.

Drill 2: Box to Base

Three teams consisting of three to four players race against each other to see who can get all three of their balls back to their starting box first. Three to four defenders will try to stop the teams from retrieving the balls from the zones. A defender may tag any player without a ball. The tagged player is frozen until a player from her team passes her a ball. A player with a ball cannot be frozen, but she can have the ball taken from her or kicked out of bounds. All balls kicked out of bounds or stolen go back to the original zone and the player who lost the ball is now frozen. If all players on a team are frozen, then they will all be free to move again at that time. The first team to get all their balls to the starting box wins the game.

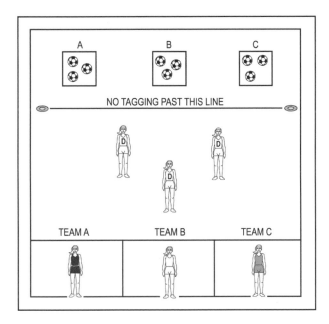

Setup: The starting boxes should be set up 30 yards from the ball zones.

Key skills learned: This game teaches players to work as a team in order to win games. Dribbling and passing are the skills most practiced in this game.

Coach's corner: The coach needs to be a referee and enforce the rules.

Alternatives to this game: Remove the team's designated ball box and allow any player to pick a ball from any of the boxes. You can also allow players to steal the balls from the players on the different teams. The team that gets the most balls back to its starting box wins the game.

Drill 3: Four Goal Glory

Four teams compete simultaneously in a fast-paced game. Each team can designate who will attack and who will defend for its team. The objective is to score a goal by dribbling the ball under control through an opponent's goal. The team that scores can take one cone back to its goal. The scoring team loses possession of the ball after the goal. The team that collects all the cones or has the most at the end of a set amount of time is the winner. If a team loses all of its cones, then the coach can decide whether that team is out of the competition or whether it can now use all of its players as offense until a cone has been won.

Setup: The size of the field will depend on how many players are on a team. Two or three soccer balls are used during this game.

Key skills learned: This game teaches the importance of switching the direction of the attack. Players will learn that if one area is blocked, it is to their advantage to choose a different area to attack. Dribbling to beat an opponent and short passing are the skills most used to complete this drill.

Coach's corner: Mark a small goal box in front of each goal to prevent players from standing on the goal line like a goalie. Keep an extra ball or two available in case one ball is kicked a long way from the field. Otherwise, it is unfair to the team that must lose a player to chase the ball. Players do not have to remain just offense or defense; they can constantly shift positions.

Alternatives to this game: Play this game as designed.

Drill 4: Two In, Two Out

Teams consist of three or four players, and will be given a number or a color. All the teams will line up around the outside of the field. It is wise to have at least one player from each team line up near both goals, in case the team needs to defend it from the other teams. A ball is thrown out into the playing field and the coach calls out the two numbers or colors which are to scrimmage. The two teams will attempt to score on either goal. The teams come off the field after a goal has been scored and await the next two teams to be called.

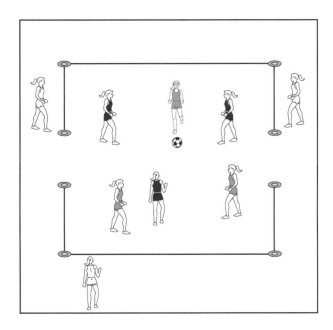

Setup: The field should be 30 yards long and 20 yards wide.

Key skills learned: This game makes the players work hard to improve their conditioning. The game is also designed to help players focus on things beyond the basic soccer game. Players must listen to the numbers being called, recover to a good position after their team has finished, and be smart about when and when not to change the direction of the attack.

Coach's corner: Players do not expect their team's number to be called back to back. By making a team play two games in a row, you increase players' fitness and keep them mentally into the game. A helpful hint to the teams is to make sure it always has at least one player near each goal. The coach should have a supply of balls near the field to keep play continuous.

Alternatives to this game: The coach can call more than two teams or, for fun, call all the teams at once.

Drill 5: World Cup

Teams that consist of two to three players are gathered around the 18-yard box. A ball is crossed into the box and each team tries to gain possession and score a goal. A goal is awarded to the team whose player was the last to touch the ball before it crossed the goal line. The player who takes the shot may not be the one who gets credit for the goal. The team that scores qualifies for the second round and will sit out until all but one team remains. The final remaining team is removed and all the teams that qualified now play a second round. This will continue until you have one winner. Rounds do not take very long, so the down time between each round should be used to gather the balls.

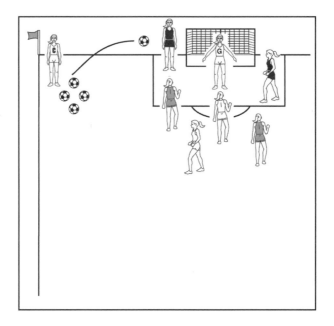

Setup: Use the 18-yard box and surrounding area for this game.

Key skills learned: This is a finishing game. Players must practice their goal-scoring abilities. The players may be asked to head, volley, dribble or shoot in order to score a goal in this game.

Coach's corner: Try to have teams that consist of players who normally play offense paired with players who normally play defense. Vary how the balls are put into play. An example would be to cross the first ball and simply pass the next ball to the corner of the 18-yard box. If you mix up how the ball is put into play, it will keep the players from being able to cheat into good positions. A key thing to remember is that the last player to *touch* the ball gets credit for the goal. It may not necessarily be the player who took the shot.

Alternatives to this game: Play this game as designed.

Drill 6: Two-Sided Goals

Teams of three or four players scrimmage on a small field. Each team can score on either goal. Players may score from the front or the back of the goal by passing the ball through the cones to a teammate on the other side of the goal. Possession is not relinquished upon scoring a goal. A team remains in possession until the other team steals the ball.

Setup: Set up two goals using flags or cones. Leave enough space behind each goal to allow for players to maneuver.

Key skills learned: This game develops a player's ability to dribble the ball past a defender and improves team passing. Players will utilize one-on-one skills and team-attacking skills.

Coach's corner: Set up as many fields as needed to include all the players. Stand in a centralized location to be able to watch all the fields without having to move to a new viewing area. Separate the players according to skill levels to ensure teams have competitive matches.

Alternatives to this drill: Coaches may want to change the number of players to increase or decrease the team size.

Drill 7: Throw, Head and Catch

Teams with equal numbers of players compete in a game of skill and strategy. Players may not move with the ball but can run without it. To advance the ball, the first player throws it to a teammate. The teammate must head the ball to a third player who then catches it. If the ball hits the ground during any part of the exchange, the other team is awarded it. The defensive team can challenge any part of the exchange, but it has to be at least two yards from the thrower. The defense must challenge with the action that is being attempted. If a player throws the ball, then the defensive player can only win the ball by challenging with a header. If the player has already headed the ball then the defense can attempt to catch the ball with her hands. Goals must be scored by a header.

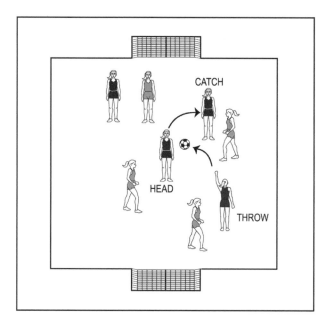

Setup: Outline a field using cones or flags. The size of the playing area depends on the number of players participating in the game.

Key skills learned: This game is designed to help the players practice individual heading skills and develop an understanding of spacing around the ball.

Coach's corner: The players must communicate in order to be successful in this game. It will take the whole team working together to score a goal. Take a minute to help players realize the proper distance from the ball they need to achieve in order to support the player with the ball.

Alternatives to this drill: Coaches can change the rules of the game to best suit the needs of their individual teams. Perhaps the game will consist of a volley-and-catch method of advancing the ball. There are many other combinations to use to improve upon the individual skills of your team.

Drill 8: Soccer Tennis

Soccer tennis is a great skills-oriented game. Teams of two compete to win a game designed to help players develop a touch on the ball. A player serves the ball in from the back line, and it must pass over the "net" (above the knee) and bounce inside the grid. The ball can only bounce one time before it must be returned over the net (above the knee). Players may juggle the ball to get an easier touch, but if the ball hits the ground at any time, then a point is given to the other team. Team passing (through the air) is allowed but the one-bounce rule is still in effect.

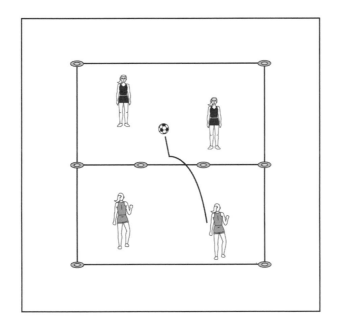

Setup: The field is outlined by cones with an imaginary net running across the center of the grid. The skill level of the players competing in the game should determine the length and width of the grid.

Key skills learned: This is an excellent game for helping players to develop a touch on the ball. Players will practice controlling the ball out of the air and passing it to an exact location. Team tactics and team communication are also improved while competing in this game.

Coach's corner: The size of the grid is the most important aspect in setting up this drill. The players must be challenged in placing the ball inside of the grid, but the grid should not be so large that the player does not need to concentrate on the pass. Set up teams of equal skill levels to play each other to ensure the teams are competitive.

Alternatives to this drill: Coaches, players and teams can decide how to score the game and how disputes in calls are settled.

Drill 9: Capture the Cone

Two teams compete in a Capture-the-Flag-style game. Balls may be passed or dribbled over the opposing team's goal line. The ball must then be stopped within the goal zone to constitute a score. The defense cannot enter the zone to prevent the player from stopping the ball. When a team successfully gets a ball into the scoring zone, the player with the ball is allowed to take one cone from the goal. Players with a cone in their hands may not pass, but are forced to dribble. They must attempt to dribble the ball back to their team's zone without losing possession of it. If the player loses control of the ball to the other team, then that player must drop the cone at the spot where possession was lost. A player from either team who is dribbling a ball may now pick up the cone. The team that gets all the cones in its goal zone wins the game.

Setup: The size of the field will depend on the number of players and their skill level. Three balls are used in this game.

Key skills learned: This is a team-building exercise that also helps players understand that they need to be aware of things happening away from the ball. Passing, dribbling and communicating are the skills practiced in this game.

Coach's corner: Help the teams by informing them of advantages gained by the other team (e.g., if a player is alone on the back side and is about to score). Pointing these out will help the players learn to look at all the areas of the field and not just to follow where the ball. Set a time limit for how long a player can wait before leaving the goal zone with the captured cone.

Alternatives to this game: Play this game as designed.

Drill 10: Team Survivor

Two teams start the game with the same number of balls in their zones. The objective is to get as many balls as possible into each team's respective goal in the center of the field. Teams score goals by passing the ball to a team player located inside the target goal. The ball must be stopped inside the goal area or it is free to be played by any player outside the goal perimeter. Outside players may not enter the goal, and target players may not leave their own team's goal. Teams may choose to take as few or as many balls outside their zone at any given time. Once a ball is taken out of the zone it can be stolen by the other team. The game ends when all the balls have been scored.

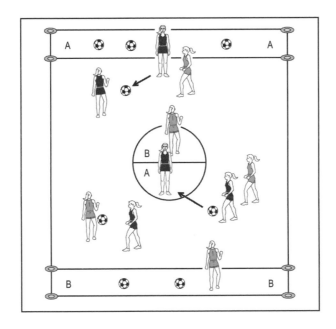

Setup: The goal areas should be no larger than 10 yards from top to bottom. The field length should be no smaller than 40 yards. This gives the players enough room for offense and defense.

Key skills learned: This game teaches players the value of utilizing a strategy in order to win games. Dribbling, passing and defending are the skills most practiced in this game.

Coach's corner: There are several ways to play this game and to change its dynamics. What happens if the team changes the number of defenders or attackers? What if you bring all the balls out of the safe area at the same time? These changes force the other team to adapt to new circumstances and to learn to defend against them. This knowledge will help the players adjust better to other teams' attacking systems and styles in a real soccer game.

Alternatives to this game: Play this game as designed.

Drill 11: Soccer Football

This game is played like Frisbee Football except the players use their feet. Teams kick off and try to intercept passes from player to player. The player receiving the pass has two yards to control the pass. If the ball is not controlled and the player does not stop movement within two yards, the ball is turned over to the other team. Players with the ball may not move from the spot where the ball was controlled. Once the ball is under control, the defending players may not get within two yards of the player with the ball. Passes, however, can be intercepted. Goals are scored when a team passes the ball into the goal zone and the ball is stopped before it rolls out of the zone. If the ball goes beyond the back of the goal zone, it is turned over to the defensive team.

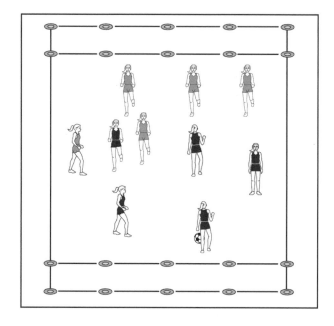

Setup: The size of the field will depend on the number of players competing in the game.

Key skills learned: This game forces the players to bring the ball under control in high-pressure situations. Players will also learn the value of a supporting pass, drop pass and lateral pass.

Coach's corner: Show the players that in order to attack in a forward direction, you sometimes need to go backward. Stop the play and point out situations where an overlapping run could benefit the player. Finally, demonstrate how important it is to get open for a pass.

Alternatives to this game: Play the game just like a scrimmage, but score in the same manner as outlined above.

Drill 12: Shooting Gallery

Two teams scrimmage each other inside of a confined area. Teams will consist of three defenders and either one or two offensive players. Defensive players cannot leave their team's defensive zone. Offensive players cannot come back across the half line. The idea of the game is to move the ball from side to side or back to front as fast as possible in order to get a clean shot on the goal. Players should be encouraged to shoot if the opportunity becomes available. Defenders need to approach the half line to challenge shots from the other team's defense. The winner is the first team to score three goals.

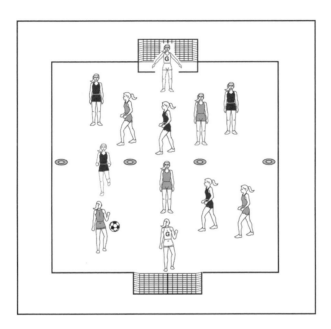

Setup: The two goals need to be no more than 30 yards apart, with a half line marked between them. This drill also requires a lot of extra balls.

Key skills learned: There is no other drill or game, in my opinion, that is a better tool for teaching players how to move the ball quickly from player to player than this game. Players will practice moving into space, passing the ball, and shooting on the goal while playing this game.

Coach's corner: The players will get the most out of this activity if they learn the secrets of the game and how they translate to the field.

1. Show them how effective it is to move the ball quickly from one outside back position all the way across to the other outside back position.

2. Demonstrate how the offensive player can open up great scoring opportunities by calling for the ball in the center of the field. The offensive player can then drop the ball left or right to a back player for an open shot.

3. Inform the center back player that if she moves for a drop pass from the left or right back, then she can immediately hit the opposite back player with a pass that gives that player a scoring opportunity. The team with the ball needs to view the half line as the 18-yard box of the defensive team. It is important that

the players are aware of this distinction, so the defense does not play the ball in front of its own goal.

Alternatives to this game: Play this game as designed.

Drill 12: Soccer Bowling

Soccer bowling is a game that focuses on the accuracy and pace of a player's passes. Players team up with one partner on each side of the "alley." Players begin the game by standing on either side of the back cone (out of play). The objective is to pass the ball into the alley and knock down the tall cones or "pins" with it. The ball must have enough power to continue forward into the partner's zone. If the ball stops in the alley, the pin is set back up. Once the ball enters the partner's zone, she can pass it back through the alley in an attempt to hit another cone. After each pass, the player that passes the ball must run around the back cone before playing the ball again. If the ball goes outside of the playing area, the players begin again at the back cone, and any pin hit by that pass is reset. The team that knocks down the most cones is the winner.

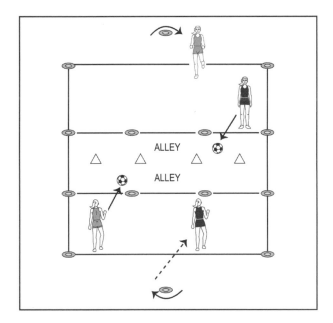

Setup: The skill level of the players participating in the game determines the size of the field.

Key skills learned: Players will improve their ability to make accurate passes while being placed under the pressure of time and space. Players will also learn the appropriate amount of pace that needs to be put on each pass to achieve their goal.

Coach's corner: Players must complete the game using one-touch passing. Make sure the players run around the cones after each pass. Coaches also need to supervise the games to ensure that no rules are being broken. Note: players are not allowed to enter the alley.

Alternatives to this drill: Instead of having teams split up on both sides of the field, teams can compete from field to field. Which team is first in knocking down all the cones?

ABOUT THE AUTHOR

Stephen McGill holds a national level "D" coaches license and was recently the head coach of girls soccer at Cambridge Academy, Inc. Stephen coachee both the high school varsity and the middle school teams. Under his leadership, the Cambridge Lady Cougars captured two conference championships in the last three years of his tenure. In 2000, Stephen coached the Cougars to their first-ever SCISA AA State Championship. The Cougars finished the season a perfect 13-0 for AA play. Stephen was also the head coach for the Toros Football Club's U-18 girls team. The "Pride" went 7-1 in 2002 and finished on top of its league.

As a player, Stephen received training from several top coaches from the United States and other countries. This training was the result of being selected to play for several Junior Olympic and state teams. Stephen was also a captain on his high school soccer team and was named to the all-tournament team in 1991. After high school, Stephen went on to play NCAA Division II soccer for Lander University in Greenwood, South Carolina.

Today Stephen and his family live in Florida.